The New Observer's Series
AIRCRAFT

About the Book

The *Observer's Book of Aircraft* is the indispensable annual pocket guide to the world's latest aeroplanes and helicopters, and most recent versions of established aircraft types. This, the thirty-fourth annual edition, embraces the latest fixed-wing and variable-geometry aeroplanes and rotorcraft of twenty-three countries. Its scope ranges from such general aviation newcomers as the Gates-Piaggio GP-180 and the Gulfstream IV, through the latest airliners, such as the Fokker 50 and ATR 42, to the newest military trainers as represented by the A-10 Wamira, the IAR 99 Soim, the Kawasaki XT-4, the Fairchild T-46, the Pilatus PC-9 and the Valmet L-80TP. The first provisional data are included of the immense An-224 *Condor* Soviet strategic transport equivalent of the USA's Lockheed Galaxy which reappears in this edition in its new C-5B version, and new variants of other established types, such as the Maritime Enforcer version of the Fokker F27 and the airborne early warning version of the Lockheed P-3 Orion, also appear in the pages that follow. All data has been checked and revised as necessary, and more than half of the three-view silhouettes are new or have been revised.

About the Author

William Green, compiler of the *Observer's Book of Aircraft* for 34 years, is internationally known for many works of aviation reference. William Green entered aviation journalism during the early years of World War II, subsequently serving with the RAF and resuming aviation writing in 1947. He is currently managing editor of one of the largest-circulation European-based aviation journals, *Air International*, and co-editor of *Air Enthusiast* and the *RAF Yearbook*.

The New Observer's Book of
Aircraft

Compiled by
William Green

with silhouettes by
Dennis Punnett

Describing 142 aircraft
with 247 illustrations

1985 edition

Frederick Warne

Penguin Books Ltd, Harmondsworth,
   Middlesex, England
Viking Penguin Inc., 40 West 23rd Street,
   New York, New York 10010, U.S.A.
Penguin Books Australia Ltd, Ringwood,
   Victoria, Australia
Penguin Books Canada Ltd, 2801 John Street,
   Markham, Ontario, Canada L3R 1B4
Penguin Books (N.Z.) Ltd, 182–190 Wairau
   Road, Auckland 10, New Zealand

Thirty-fourth edition 1985

ISBN 0 7232 1687 8

Printed in Great Britain by Butler & Tanner
Ltd, Frome and London

INTRODUCTION TO THE 1985 EDITION

SINCE, thirty-four years ago, the *Observer's Book of Aircraft* first became an annual publication, each successive edition has generated letters whose authors have decried the omission of aircraft types that they frequently see on airfields or in the skies of the particular part of the world in which they reside. It has therefore become necessary to reiterate, from time to time, the *raison d'être* of this book.

Unlike most contemporary source books, the *Observer's Book of Aircraft* is not devoted primarily to those aeroplanes that are *numerically* most important or are most likely to be *seen* in the world's skies. All such *have* appeared in past editions. If extent of usage or quantitative factors be accepted as the criterion for inclusion or exclusion of specific aircraft types, not only would a volume of this size be rendered impracticable, but the content of the *Observer's Book of Aircraft* would change insufficiently from year to year to warrant an annual edition.

Primacy in this book is given to the most recent aircraft types to appear and to the newest variants of established production types that have entered flight test in the preceding year or are scheduled to fly during the year of the volume's currency. The *force majeure* of finding space for débutantes on the world aviation scene dictates the discarding from each yearly edition of *some* aircraft that still retain production significance, although such are reinstated if and when they appear in new form. A case in point is the Lockheed P-3 Orion maritime aircraft which appeared in every successive edition from 1960 until 1982, and reappears in the following pages in airborne early warning form which entered flight test last year. Again, some aircraft that have passed from production and have, accordingly, been deleted from the annual edition, are reinstated when production is resumed, as, for example, the Lockheed C-5 Galaxy strategic transport.

With each successive edition of the *Observer's Book of Aircraft*, the data given for aircraft that reappear are updated in the light of information provided by their manufacturers or gleaned from intelligence sources. The accompanying general arrangement silhouette drawings are carefully checked to cater for any modifications or changes that may have been applied to the aircraft concerned. In this edition, more than half of the drawings are either new to this publication or have been revised since they last appeared.

Thus, the *Observer's Book of Aircraft* endeavours to provide, in as compact a form as possible, a continuous record of aircraft design development in all the principal categories.

WILLIAM GREEN

AAC A 10 WAMIRA

Country of Origin: Australia.
Type: Side-by-side two-seat basic trainer.
Power Plant: One 550 shp Pratt & Whitney (Canada) PT6A-25D turboprop.
Performance: (Manufacturer's estimates) Max speed, 234 mph (376 km/h) at 15,000 ft (4 570 m); max cruise, 207 mph (333 km/h) at sea level; max initial climb, 1,840 ft/min (9,35 m/sec); time to 10,000 ft (3 050 m), 5·5 min; endurance (with 50 min reserves), 3 hr.
Weights: Empty equipped, 3,073 lb (1 394 kg); loaded (normal training mission), 4,409 lb (2 000 kg); max take-off (utility), 5,732 lb (2 600 kg).
Status: First of two prototypes scheduled to enter flight test summer 1985. RAAF requirement for 69 aircraft with deliveries commencing 1987–88.
Notes: The Wamira has been designed to meet the requirements of RAAF specification AC180 and is being built by the Australian Aircraft Consortium formed by Commonwealth Aircraft, the Government Aircraft Factories and Hawker de Havilland. The Wamira is intended to replace the piston-engined CT4 primary/basic trainer and, eventually, the MB-326H jet basic/advanced trainer in the RAAF pilot training curriculum. During 1984, a proposed tandem two-seat derivative with a more powerful PT6A-25C engine was unsuccessfully tendered to meet the RAF's AST 412 trainer requirement as the A 20. The Wamira has provision for four wing hardpoints stressed for loads up to 551 lb (250 kg) inboard and 330 lb (150 kg) outboard. The AAC possesses no production facilities and manufacture will be distributed between the companies participating in the venture.

AAC A 10 WAMIRA

Dimensions: Span, 36 ft 1 in (11,00 m); length, 32 ft 10 in (10,01 m); height, 12 ft 1⅝ in (3,70 m); wing area, 215·3 sq ft (20,00 m²).

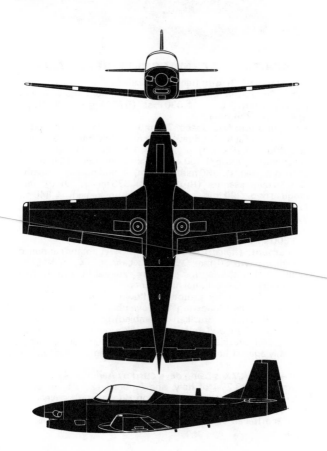

AERITALIA-AERMACCHI-EMBRAER AMX

Countries of Origin: Italy and Brazil.
Type: Single-seat battlefield support and light attack aircraft.
Power Plant: One 11,030 lb st (5 000 kgp) Rolls-Royce Spey Mk 807 turbofan.
Performance: Max speed, 720 mph (1 160 km/h) at 1,000 ft (305 m) or Mach=0·95; average cruise, 590 mph (950 km/h) at 2,000 ft (610 km/h) or Mach=0.77; combat radius (LO-LO-LO with 3,000 lb/1 360 kg ordnance and two 110 Imp gal/500 l drop tanks), 230 mls (370 km) including 5 min combat and 10 min reserves, (HI-LO-LO-HI) 323 mls (520 km); ferry range (two 220 Imp gal/1 000 l drop tanks), 1,840 mls (2 965 km).
Weights: Operational empty, 13,228 lb (6 000 kg); typical mission, 23,700 lb (10 750 kg); max take-off, 25,353 lb (11 500 kg).
Armament: (Italian) One 20-mm M61A1 rotary cannon or (Brazilian) two 30-mm DEFA 553 cannon, two AIM-9L or similar AAMs at wingtips and max external load of 7,716 lb (3 500 kg) on five external hardpoints.
Status: First of six prototypes flown 15 May 1984, with second and third following 19 November 1984 and 28 January 1985. Fourth (Brazilian-assembled) prototype scheduled to fly July 1985, and anticipated peak production (combined Italian and Brazilian assembly lines) planned at 10 aircraft monthly against Italian and Brazilian requirements for 187 and 79.
Notes: The AMX is being developed by Aeritalia (47·1%) and Aermacchi (23·2%) of Italy, and Embraer (29·7%) of Brazil. There is no component production duplication between the participating manufacturers, the Brazilian version differing from the Italian version in armament, weapons systems and avionics.

AERITALIA-AERMACCHI-EMBRAER AMX

Dimensions: Span, 29 ft 1½ in (8,87 m); length, 44 ft 6½ in (13,57 m); height, 15 ft 0¼ in (4,58 m); wing area, 226·05 sq ft (21,00 m²).

AERMACCHI MB-339A

Country of Origin: Italy.

Type: Tandem two-seat basic and advanced trainer.

Power Plant: One 4,000 lb st (1 814 kgp) Fiat-built Rolls-Royce Viper 632-43 or (MB-339B) 4,580 lb st (2 077 kgp) Viper 680–43 turbojet.

Performance: (Viper 632-43) Max speed, 558 mph (898 km/h) at sea level, 508 mph (817 km/h) at 30,000 ft (9 145 m); initial climb, 6,195 ft/min (33,5 m/sec); service ceiling, 48,000 ft (14 630 m); max range (internal fuel with 10% reserves), 1,093 mls (1 760 km).

Weights: Empty, 6,780 lb (3 075) kg); normal loaded, 9,700 lb (4 400 kg); max take-off, 13,000 lb (5 897 kg).

Armament: (Training and light strike) Up to 4,000 lb (1 815 kg) of ordnance between six underwing stations.

Status: First of two prototypes flown 12 August 1976, with deliveries to Italian Air Force commencing February 1981, these being preceded by first export deliveries (10 for Argentine Navy) commencing November 1980. Orders for Italian Air Force totalled 101, export orders including 12 for Malaysia, 12 for Nigeria, four for Dubai and 16 for Peru.

Notes: The uprated Viper 680-43 entered flight test in the MB-339A late June 1983, and production aircraft with this engine will be available during 1985 as the MB-339B. This engine is also being proposed for the single-seat light close air support version, the MB-339K Veltro 2 (see 1981 edition) which was fitted with a head-up display and an inertial nav/attack system during 1984. The 100th production MB-339 was completed mid-May 1983. Plans to assemble and part-manufacture 50 MB-339As and MB-339Ks in Peru were in abeyance at the beginning of 1985.

AERMACCHI MB-339A

Dimensions: Span, 35 ft 7 in (10,86 m); length, 36 ft 0 in (10,97 m); height, 13 ft 1 in (3,99 m); wing area, 207·74 sq ft (19,30 m²).

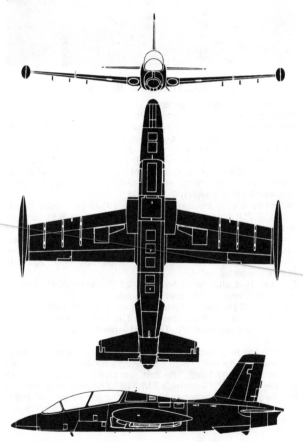

AEROSPATIALE TB 30 EPSILON

Country of Origin: France.

Type: Tandem two-seat primary/basic trainer.

Power Plant: One 300 hp Avco Lycoming AEIO-540-L1B5-D six-cylinder horizontally-opposed engine.

Performance: (At max take-off weight) Max speed, 236 mph (380 km/h) at sea level; max cruise (75% power), 222 mph (358 km/h) at 6,000 ft (1 830 m); max initial climb, 1,850 ft/min (9,4 m/sec); service ceiling, 23,000 ft (7 010 m); endurance (60% power), 3·75 hrs.

Weights: Empty equipped, 2,922 lb (917 kg); loaded (aerobatic), 2,756 lb (1 250 kg); max take-off, 3,086 lb (1 400 kg).

Armament: (Export) Four underwing hardpoints stressed to carry 352 lb (160 kg) inboard and 176 lb (80 kg) outboard. Alternative loads include two twin 7,62-mm machine gun pods, four six-rocket (68-mm) pods, or two 264·5-lb (120 kg) bombs.

Status: Two prototypes flown on 22 December 1979 and 12 July 1980 respectively, and first production Epsilon flown on 29 June 1983. Sixty ordered by beginning of 1985 against total *Armée de l' Air* requirement for 150, production rate at that time being three monthly. Three of armed version ordered by Togo.

Notes: The first six series Epsilons were delivered to the *Armée de l' Air* in June 1984, with the 150th aircraft scheduled to be delivered in July 1988. The first prototype is being modified to take a 350 shp Turboméca TM 319 turboprop with which it is scheduled to commence flight tests in the autumn of 1985. The airframe of the Epsilon is not expected to demand any major modification for conversion from piston engine to turboprop.

AEROSPATIALE TB 30 EPSILON

Dimensions: Span 25 ft 11½ in (7,92 m); length, 24 ft 10½ in (7,59 m); height, 8 ft 8¾ in (2,66 m); wing area, 103·34 sq ft (9,60 m²).

AEROSPATIALE-AERITALIA ATR 42

Countries of Origin: France and Italy.
Type: Regional airliner.
Power Plant: Two 1,800 shp Pratt & Whitney (Canada) PW120 turboprops.
Performance: (Manufacturer's estimates) Max cruise speed, 320 mph (515 km/h) at 20,000 ft (6 095 m); max initial climb, 1,860 ft/min (9,45 m/sec); cruise ceiling, 25,000 ft (7 620 m); max range (46 passengers and reserves), 1,094 mls (1 760 km), (max fuel and reserves), 2,878 mls (4 633 km).
Weights: Operational empty, 21,206 lb (9 619 kg); max take-off, 34,725 lb (15 750 kg).
Accommodation: Crew of two on flight deck with optional third seat, and alternative seating arrangements for 42, 46, 48 or 50 passengers in four-abreast seating with central aisle.
Status: First and second prototypes flown on 16 August and 31 October respectively, with certification scheduled for late summer of 1985. First deliveries expected to commence in November 1985, and 11 ATR 42s are scheduled to have flown by the end of the year, with 39 having flown by the end of 1986. Orders and options totalled approximately 70 aircraft by the beginning of 1985.
Notes: The ATR (*Avion de Transport Régional*) 42 is being developed jointly by Aérospatiale of France and Aeritalia of Italy on a 50-50 basis. Several derivatives of the basic design are projected, including a stretched version of 60-66 passengers with deliveries commencing 1988–89, a military freighter, the ATM 42, with rear loading facilities and a maritime patrol variant, the ATM 42-S. The latter will feature specialised search radar and have the ability to carry two AM 39 Exocet anti-ship missiles.

AEROSPATIALE-AERITALIA ATR 42

Dimensions: Span, 80 ft 7⅓ in (24,57 m); length, 74 ft 5½ in (22,67 m); height, 24 ft 10¾ in (7,59 m); wing area, 586·65 sq ft (54·50 m²).

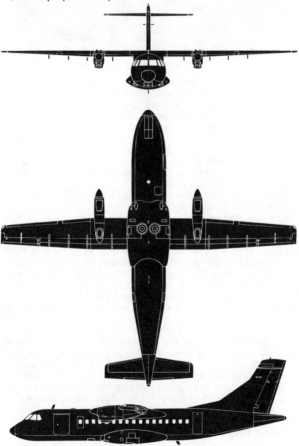

AIRBUS A300-600

Country of Origin: International consortium.

Type: Medium-haul commercial airliner.

Power Plant: Two 56,000 lb st (25 400 kgp) Pratt & Whitney JT9D-7R4H1 or General Electric CF6-80C2 turbofans.

Performance: Max cruise speed, 554 mph (891 km/h) at 31,000 ft (9 450 m); econ cruise, 536 mph (862 km/h) at 33,000 ft (10 060 m); range cruise, 518 mph (833 km/h) at 35,000 ft (10 670 m); range (max payload), 3,430 mls (5 200 km) at econ cruise, (max fuel with 52,900-lb/23 995-kg payload), 5,320 mls (8 560 km).

Weights: Operational empty, 193,410 lb (87 728 kg); max take-off, 363,760 lb (165,000 kg).

Accommodation: Flight crew of three and maximum seating for 344 passengers, a typical arrangement being for 267 passengers in a mixed-class layout.

Status: First A300-600 flown on 8 July 1983, and certified on 9 March 1984, with first customer delivery (to Saudia) following in May. Total of 251 A300s (all versions) ordered by 1985 when 242 delivered. Production rate (including A310) three per month at beginning of 1985.

Notes: The A300 is manufactured by a consortium of Aérospatiale (France), British Aerospace (UK), Deutsche Airbus (Federal Germany) and CASA (Spain). The latest version, the A300-600, replaces the A300B4-200 (see 1983 edition) from which if differs primarily in having the new, re-profiled rear fuselage of the A310 with an extension of the parallel portion of the fuselage offering an 18-seat increase in passenger capacity, and later-generation engines as offered with the A310. The first CF6-80C2-powered -600 will be delivered to the launch customer, Thai International, during the autumn of 1985, and the extended-range A300-600ER will be introduced in 1986.

AIRBUS A300-600

Dimensions: Span, 147 ft 1¼ in (44,84 m); length, 177 ft 5 in (54,08 m); height, 54 ft 3 in (16,53 m); wing area, 2,799 sq ft (260,00 m²).

AIRBUS A310-200

Country of Origin: International consortium.

Type: Short/medium-haul commercial airliner.

Power Plant: Two 48,000 lb st (21 800 kgp) General Electric CF6-80A1 or Pratt & Whitney JT9D-7R4D1, or 50,000 lb st (22 680 kgp) CF6-80A3 or JT9D-7R4E1 turbofans.

Performance: Max cruise speed, 562 mph (904 km/h) at 33,000 ft (10 060 m); econ cruise, 528 mph (850 km/h) at 37,000 ft (11 280 m); long-range cruise, 522 mph (840 km/h) at 39,000 ft (11 885 m); range (236 passengers), 2,995 mls (4 820 km), (max payload), 1,440 mls (2 315 km).

Weights: Operational empty (typical), 175,863 lb (79 770 kg); max take-off, 291,010 lb (132 000 kg), (option), 305,560 lb (138 600 kg).

Accommodation: Flight crew of two or three with single-class seating for 236 or 262 passengers eight abreast, or (typical mixed-class) 20 first-class six-abreast and 200 economy-class eight abreast.

Status: First A310 flown on 3 April 1982, with first customer delivery (to Swissair) spring 1983. Total of 109 A310s ordered by beginning of 1985, when production rate (including A300—see pages 16–17) was three monthly, with 29 A310s delivered during 1984 and 45 in service by beginning of 1985.

Notes: By comparison with the earlier A300B, the A310 has a new, higher aspect ratio wing, a shorter fuselage, a new, smaller tailplane and a new undercarriage, but retains a high degree of commonality with the preceding and larger aircraft. Like the A300B, the A310 is being built by a consortium of French, British, Federal German and Spanish companies. The longer-range A310-300 (ordered by Swissair) will be delivered from late 1985, having an effective range (with 218 passengers) of 4,605 mls (7 410 km).

AIRBUS A310-200

Dimensions: Span, 144 ft 0 in (43,90 m); length, 153 ft 1 in (46,66 m); height, 51 ft 10 in (15,81 m); wing area, 2,357·3 sq ft (219,00 m²).

ANTONOV AN-32 (CLINE)

Country of origin: USSR.
Type: Military tactical transport.
Power Plant: Two 4,195 ehp Ivchenko Al-20M or 5,180 ehp Al-20DM turboprops.
Performance: (Al-20DM engines) Normal continuous cruise, 329 mph (530 km/h) at 26,250 ft (8 000 m); service ceiling, 29,525 ft (9 000 m); range with 45 min reserves (max fuel), 1,367 mls (2 200 km), (max payload), 487 mls (800 km).
Weights: (Al-20DM engines) Max take-off, 59,525 lb (27 000 kg).
Accommodation: Flight crew of five and 39 troops on tip-up seats along fuselage sides, 30 fully-equipped paratroops or 24 casualty stretchers and one medical attendant. A max of 14,770 lb (6 700 kg) of freight may be carried.
Status: Based on the An-26 (Curl), the An-32 was first flown in prototype form late 1976, production of a more powerful version (Al-20DM engines) developed specifically to meet an Indian requirement being initiated in 1982. Deliveries against an Indian order for 95 aircraft commenced in July 1984.
Notes: The Al-20DM-powered An-32 is intended specifically for operation under high temperature conditions or from high-altitude airfields. It features triple-slotted wing trailing-edge flaps and automatic leading-edge slats, and has low-pressure tyres to permit operation from unpaved strips. Named Sutlej (after the Punjabi river) in Indian Air Force service, the An-32 is reported to have been ordered by Tanzania, but the only major customer announced by the beginning of 1985 was India. The An-32 can accommodate various small wheeled or tracked vehicles which may be airdropped via a rear loading hatch and forward-sliding ramp-door.

ANTONOV AN-32 (CLINE)

Dimensions: Span, 95 ft 9½ in (29,20 m); length, 77 ft 8¼ in (23,68 m); height, 28 ft 8½ in (8,75 m); wing area, 807·1 sq ft (74,98 m²).

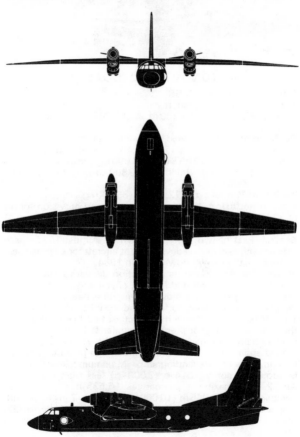

ANTONOV AN-72 (COALER)

Country of Origin: USSR.
Type: STOL utility transport.
Power Plant: Two 14,330 lb st (6 500 kgp) Lotarev D-36 turbofans.
Performance: Max speed, 472 mph (760 km/h); max continuous cruise, 447 mph (720 km/h); normal operating altitudes, 26,250-32,800 ft (8 000–10 000 m); range with 30 min reserves (max fuel), 2,360 mls (3 800 km), (max payload), 620 mls (1 000 km).
Weights: Max take-off, 72,750 lb (33 000 kg).
Accommodation: Flight crew of three and provision for up to 32 passengers on fold-down seats along cabin sides, or 24 casualty stretchers plus medical attendant.
Status: First of two protypes flown 31 August 1977, these subsequently serving as development aircraft for a refined series version, the An-74, flown early in 1984.
Notes: The An-72 and its production derivative, the An-74, achieve short take-off and landing characteristics (STOL) by means of upper surface blowing, engine exhaust gases flowing over the upper wing surfaces and the inboard slotted flaps. The series An-74, of which few details had been revealed at the time of closing for press, has similar D-36 turbofans and is essentially a refined version of the An-72, having an extended span and a wheel-ski undercarriage permitting operation on snow and ice landing strips. Maximum take-off weight is quoted as some 6,614 lb (3 000 kg) less than that of the An-72, and maximum payload as 16,535 lb (7 500 kg) as compared with 22,045 lb (10 000 kg). The An-74 is fitted with a special ramp-door essentially similar to that of the An-32, permitting wheeled or tracked vehicles to be driven into the hold.

ANTONOV AN-72 (COALER)

Dimensions: Span, 84 ft 9 in (25,83 m); length, 87 ft 2½ in (26,58 m); height, 27 ft 0¼ in (8,23 m); wing area, 969 sq ft (90 000 m²).

ANTONOV AN-224 (CONDOR)

Country of origin: USSR.

Type: Heavy strategic freighter.

Power Plant: Four 51,650 lb st (23 430 kgp) Lotarev D-18T turbofans.

Performance: (Estimated) Max speed, 560 mph (900 km/h) at 21,325 ft (6 500 m); max continuous cruise, 540 mph (870 km/h) at 26,245 ft (8 000 m); econ cruise, 510 mph (820 km/h); range (with max payload), 2,110 mls (3 400 km).

Weights: (Estimated) Max take-off, 850,000 lb (385 560 kg).

Accommodation: Flight crew of five-six and up to 345 fully-equipped troops, 270 paratroops or up to 275,575 lb (125 000 kg) of freight. The An-224 can reportedly accommodate all elements of the SS-20 mobile intermediate-range ballistic missile system and the largest Soviet tanks.

Status: The flight testing of the first of several prototypes reportedly commenced during the course of 1983, with production deliveries expected to commence in 1986 and initial operational capability in 1987–88.

Notes: Closely comparable with the Lockheed C-5B Galaxy (see pages 136–7) and thus one of the largest contemporary aeroplanes in the world, the An-224 is intended as a replacement for the An-22 (Cock) strategic freighter in Soviet Air Force service. The accompanying illustrations and data are provisional, the former giving no more than a general impression of the anticipated appearance of this aircraft. The main undercarriage units are believed to each comprise five pairs of wheels in tandem, the nose member possessing four wheels abreast. There is as yet no evidence of any provision for nose loading although such is considered likely.

ANTONOV AN-224 (CONDOR)

Dimensions: (Estimated) Span, 225 ft (68,60 m); length, 220 ft (67,00 m).

AVTEK 400

Country of Origin: USA.

Type: Light corporate transport.

Power Plant: Two (prototype) 680 shp Pratt & Whitney (Canada) PT6A-28 or (production) 750 shp PT6A-135 turboprops.

Performance: (Manufacturer's estimates) Max cruise speed (prototype) 415 mph (668 km/h) at 25,000 ft (7 620 m), (production), 426 mph (686 km/h) at 37,000 ft (11 280 m); econ cruise (prototype), 300 mph (483 km/h) at 33,000 ft (10 050 m); initial climb, (prototype) 5,226 ft/min (26,55 m/sec), (production), 5,400 ft/min (27,43 m/sec); range (production) at econ cruise, 2,602 mls (4 188 km).

Weights: (Manufacturer's estimates) Empty equipped (prototype), 3,014 lb (1 368 kg); max take-off (production), 5,500 lb (2 495 kg).

Accommodation: Pilot and co-pilot/passenger on flight deck and optional arrangements for four to seven passengers in main cabin.

Status: Prototype flown 17 September 1984, with deposit-paid options on 120 aircraft placed by beginning of 1985. Four production-certifiable aircraft to be built with certification schedule for 1986.

Notes: Constructed virtually entirely of Du Pont Kevlar aramid fibre composite skins with a Nomex honeycomb filling and graphite reinforcement where necessary, the Avtek 400 is of highly unconventional configuration. Components will be manufactured by the Japanese Toray concern for US final assembly, and the series version will have an oval (rather than circular) section fuselage which will incorporate a 38-in (96,5-cm) stretch.

AVTEK 400

Dimensions: (Prototype) Span, 34 ft 0 in (10,36 m); length, 34 ft 0 in (10,36 m); height, 10 ft 1 in (3,07 m); wing area 141 sq ft (13,10 m²).

BEECHCRAFT 1900

Country of Origin: USA.

Type: (1900) Regional airliner, (1900C) convertible passenger and freight transport, and (1900 Executive) corporate transport.

Power Plant: Two (flat-rated) 1,100 shp Pratt & Whitney (Canada) PT6A-65B turboprops.

Performance: Max cruising speed (at 15,000 lb/6 804 kg), 302 mph (486 km/h) at 8,000 ft (2 440 m), 275 mph (443 km/h) at 25,000 ft (7 620 m); max initial climb, 2,330 ft/min (11,84 m/sec); max range, 856 mls (1 378 km) at 16,000 ft (4 875 m), 992 mls (1 596 km) at 25,000 ft (7 620 m).

Weights: Empty, 8,700 lb (3 946 kg); max take-off, 16,600 lb (7 530 kg).

Accommodation: Flight crew of two and (1900) 19 passengers two abreast with central aisle, or (1900 Executive) typical seating for eight to fourteen passengers, the latter having six seats in forward cabin and eight seats in aft cabin. The 1900C has upward-hinging cargo door in lieu of rear passenger door.

Status: First of three prototypes flown on 3 September 1982, with certification following on 22 November 1983. Service entry (with Bar Harbour) in February 1984, with 25th aircraft delivered on 19 November of that year. Production tempo was rising from three to four aircraft monthly at the beginning of 1985.

Notes: The Beechcraft 1900 is a derivative of the King Air 200 corporate transport with which it has approximately 40 per cent commonality of component parts. Tailets projecting beneath the tailplane increase longitudinal stability and stabilons on the rear fuselage improve pitch stability and provide positive recovery from deep stalls.

BEECHCRAFT 1900

Dimensions: Span, 54 ft 6 in (16,61 m); length, 57 ft 10 in (17,63 m); height, 14 ft 10¾ in (4,53 m); wing area, 303 sq ft (28,15 m²).

BOEING 737-300

Country of Origin: USA.

Type: Short-haul commercial airliner.

Power Plant: Two 20,000 lb st (9072 kgp) General Electric CFM56-3-B1 turbofans.

Performance: Max cruising speed, 558 mph (899 km/h) at 25,000 ft (7620 m); econ cruise, 489 mph (787 km/h) at 35,000 ft (10670 m); range cruise, 495 mph (797 km/h) at 35,000 ft (10670 m); max range at econ cruise (max payload), 2,625 mls (4225 km), (max fuel), 3,408 mls (5485 km).

Weights: Operational empty, 69,580 lb (31561 kg); max take-off, 135,000 lb (61236 kg).

Accommodation: Flight crew of two and alternative arrangements for 110 to 149 passengers, typical arrangements including mixed class with four-abreast seating for eight first class and six-abreast seating for 114 or 120 tourist class passengers, or one class arrangement for 132, 140 or 149 tourist class passengers.

Status: First Model 737-300 flown on 24 February 1984, with second on 2 March 1984. First customer delivery (to US Air) 28 November 1984, and total of 160 ordered by 14 customers by beginning of 1985, when 1,254 of all models of the Model 737 had been ordered.

Notes: The Model 737-300 differs from the -200 (see 1983 edition) in having new engines, a 104-in (2,64-m) overall "stretch", strengthened wings and modified wingtips. The -300 is not simply a stretched and re-engined version of the Model 737 as it embodies many of the developments made available by the Model 757 and 767 programmes, and it is seen as complementary to the Model 737-200 rather than as a replacement, production of the earlier version continuing in parallel. At the beginning of 1985, consideration was being given to a further "stretch" to raise seating to 150 passengers.

BOEING 737-300

Dimensions: Span, 94 ft 9 in (28,90 m); length, 109 ft 7 in (33,40 m); height, 36 ft 6 in (11,12 m); wing area, 980 sq ft (91,04 m²).

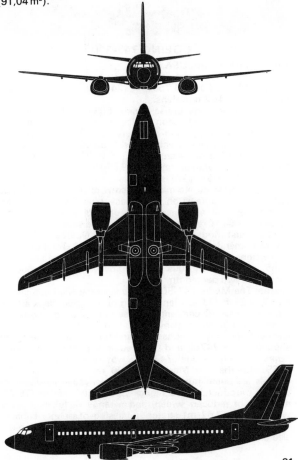

BOEING 747-300

Country of Origin: USA.

Type: Long-haul commercial airliner.

Power Plant: Four 54,750 lb st (24 835 kgp) Pratt & Whitney JT9D-7R4G2 turbofans.

Performance: Max cruise speed, 583 mph (939 km/h) at 35,000 ft (10 670 m); econ cruise, 564 mph (907 km/h) at 35,000 ft (10 670 m); long-range cruise, 558 mph (898 km/h); range (max payload at econ cruise), 6,860 mls (11 040 km), (max fuel at long-range cruise), 8,606 mls (13 850 km).

Weights: Operational empty, 389,875 lb (176 847 kg); max take-off, 833,000 lb (377 850 kg).

Accommodation: Normal flight crew of three and up to 69 passengers six-abreast on upper deck, plus basic mixed-class arrangement for 410 passengers, or 415 passengers nine-abreast or 484 10-abreast in economy class seating.

Status: First Model 747-300 flown on 5 October 1982, with first customer delivery (Swissair) March 1983. Total of 641 of all versions of the Model 747 ordered by the beginning of 1985, including 49 -300s, with 610 delivered and production running at two per month.

Notes: The Model 747-300 differs from the -200 primarily in having a 23-ft (7,0-m) lengthening of the upper deck affording a (typical) 10 per cent increase in total accommodation. Boeing is offering to convert existing Model 747s to -300 standard, the only versions that cannot be modified being the short-fuselage 747SP and those equipped with nose loading doors. The first Model 747-100 was flown on 9 February 1969, and the first Model 747-200 on 11 October 1970. Studies are being pursued of several derivative versions, including introduction of a higher aspect ratio, 250-ft (76,20-m) wing of reduced sweep, and a range of fuselage sizes, with a 25-ft (7,62-m) stretch increasing passenger capacity to a maximum of 650. A new full-length upper deck cabin is also under consideration.

BOEING 747-300

Dimensions: Span, 195 ft 8 in (59,64 m); length, 231 ft 4 in (70,51 m); height, 63 ft 5 in (19,33 m); wing area, 5,685 sq ft (528,15 m²).

BOEING 757-200

Country of Origin: USA.

Type: Short/medium-haul commercial airliner.

Power Plant: Two 37,500 lb st (17 010 kgp) Rolls-Royce RB.211-535C, 38,200 lb st (17 327 kgp) Pratt & Whitney 2037 or 40,100 lb st (18 190 kgp) Rolls-Royce RB.211-535E4 turbofans.

Performance: (RB.211-535C engines) Max cruise speed, 570 mph (917 km/h) at 30,000 ft (9 145 m); econ cruise, 528 mph (850 km/h) at 39,000 ft (11 885 m); range (max payload), 2,210 mls (3 556 km) at econ cruise, (max fuel), 5,343 mls (8 598 km) at long-range cruise.

Weights: Operational empty, 128,450 lb (58 265 kg); max take-off (RB.211-535C engines), 220,000 lb (99 790 kg).

Accommodation: Flight crew of two (with provision for optional third crew member) and typical arrangement of 178 mixed class or 196 tourist class passengers, with max single-class seating for 239 passengers.

Status: First Model 757 flown on 19 February 1982, with first customer deliveries (to Eastern) December 1982 and (British Airways) January 1983. Orders totalling 139 aircraft at beginning of 1985, of which 84 to be powered by Pratt & Whitney engines with deliveries having commenced (to Delta Air Lines) October 1984. Production rate of one-and-a-half aircraft monthly at beginning of 1985, with total of 45 delivered.

Notes: Two versions of the Model 757 are currently on offer, one with a max take-off weight of 220,000 lb (99 790 kg) and the other for post-1984 delivery with a max take-off weight of 240,000 lb (108 864 kg). The Model 757 is of narrowbody configuration and its wing has been optimised for short-haul routes. At the beginning of 1985, Boeing was engaged in studies of a combi version with a rear freight door, and a freighter and a convertible, both with forward freight doors. A PW2037-powered aircraft is illustrated above.

BOEING 757-200

Dimensions: Span, 124 ft 6 in (37,82 m); length, 155 ft 3 in (47,47 m); height, 44 ft 6 in (13,56 m); wing area, 1,951 sq ft (181,25 m²).

BOEING 767-200

Country of Origin: USA.

Type: Medium-haul commercial airliner.

Power Plant: Two 48,000 lb st (21 773 kgp) Pratt & Whitney JT9D-7R4D or General Electric CF6-80A turbofans.

Performance: (JT9D-7R4D engines) Max cruise speed, 556 mph (895 km/h) at 39,000 ft (11 890 m); econ cruise, 528 mph (850 km/h) at 39,000 ft (11 890 m); range (with max payload and no reserves), 2,717 mls (4 373 km) at econ cruise, (max fuel), 6,680 mls (10 750 km).

Weights: (JT9D-7R4D engines) Operational empty, 179,580 lb (81 457 kg); max take-off, 300,000 lb (136 080 kg).

Accommodation: Flight crew of two (with optional three-crew arrangement) and typical mixed-class seating for 18 six-abreast and 193 seven-abreast with two aisles, with max single-class seating for 290 passengers eight-abreast.

Status: First Model 767 (JT9D-7R4D engines) flown on 26 September 1981, (CF6-80A engines) 19 February 1982. First customer delivery (to United) on 18 August 1982, and 104 delivered by beginning of 1985, when 188 were on order.

Notes: Three basic versions of the Model 767 were on offer at the beginning of 1985 with 300,000 lb (136 080 kg), 315,000 lb (142 884 kg) and 335,000 lb (151 956 kg) max. take-off weights, the last-mentioned version having 50,000 lb st (22 680 kg) CF6-80A2 engines and a max volume payload range of 4,000 mls (6 437 km). Several variants are under development, including a stretched model, the 767-300 with a fuselage lengthened by 21 ft 1 in (6,43 m) and deliveries (to Japan Air Lines) to commence September 1986, and a freighter, weights up to 360,000 lb (163 296 kg) being possible with the present wing and 55,000 lb st (24 948 kgp) engines. The longer-range 767-200ER has been ordered by Ethiopian Airlines, Japan Air Lines, Air Canada, Qantas and the Egyptian government, with first delivery (to Ethiopian) in May 1984.

BOEING 767-200

Dimensions: Span, 156 ft 4 in (47,65 m); length, 159 ft 2 in (48,50 m); height, 52 ft 0 in (15,85 m); wing area, 3,050 sq ft (283,3 m²).

BOEING E-3 SENTRY

Country of Origin: USA.

Type: Airborne warning and control system aircraft.

Power Plant: Four 21,000 lb st (9 525 kgp) Pratt & Whitney TF33-PW-100A turbofans.

Performance: (At max weight) Average cruise speed, 479 mph (771 km/h) at 28,900-40,100 ft (8 810-12 220 m); average loiter speed, 376 mph (605 km/h) at 29,000 ft (8 840 m); time on station (unrefuelled) at 1,150 mls (1 850 km) from base, 6 hrs, (with one refuelling), 14·4 hrs; ferry range, 5,034 mls (8 100 km) at 475 mph (764 km/h).

Weights: Empty, 170,277 lb (77 238 kg); normal loaded, 214,300 lb (97 206 kg); max take-off, 325,000 lb (147 420 kg).

Accommodation: Operational crew of 17 comprising flight crew of four, systems maintenance team of four, a battle commander and an air defence team of eight.

Status: First of two (EC-137D) development aircraft flown 9 February 1972, two pre-production E-3As following in 1975. First 24 delivered to USAF as E-3As being modified to E-3B standards, and final 10 (including updated third test aircraft) were delivered as E-3Cs. Eighteen being delivered (in similar configuration to E-3C) to NATO as E-3As with completion June 1985. Five CFM56-powered aircraft being delivered to Saudi Arabia from August 1985.

Notes: Aircraft initially delivered to USAF as E-3As have now been fitted with JTIDS (Joint Tactical Information Distribution System), ECM-resistant voice communications, additional HF and UHF radios, austere maritime surveillance capability and more situation display consoles as E-3Bs. The E-3C featured most E-3B modifications at the production stage, and the E-3As being delivered to NATO are of similar configuration to that of the USAF's E-3C.

BOEING E-3 SENTRY

Dimensions: Span, 145 ft 9 in (44,42 m); length, 152 ft 11 in (46,61 m); height, 42 ft 5 in (12,93 m); wing area, 2,892 sq ft (268,67 m²).

BRITISH AEROSPACE 125-800

Country of Origin: United Kingdom.

Type: Light corporate executive transport.

Power Plant: Two 4,300 lb st (1 950 kgp) Garrett TFE731-5R-1H turbofans.

Performance: Max cruising speed, 533 mph (858 km/h) at 29,000 ft (8 840 m); econ cruise, 461 mph (741 km/h) at 39,000–43,000 ft (11 900–13 100 m); max initial climb, 3,100 ft/min (15,75 m/sec); service ceiling, 43,000 ft (13 100 m); range (max payload), 3,305 mls (5 318 km), (max fuel with VFR reserves), 3,454 mls (5 560 km).

Weights: Operational empty (typical), 15,120 lb (6 858 kg); max take-off, 27,400 lb (12 430 kg).

Accommodation: Pilot and co-pilot on flight deck with seat for third crew member, and standard arrangement for eight passengers in main cabin with optional arrangements for up to 14 seats.

Status: Prototype of 800 series 125 flown on 26 May 1983, with type certification being achieved in May 1984. Production rate expected to rise from two to three per month during 1985, 25 800 series aircraft having been sold by the beginning of the year.

Notes: The BAe 125-800 is an extensively revised development of the -700 (see 1982 edition) with more powerful engines, new, longer-span outboard wing sections, new ailerons, redesigned flight deck and larger ventral fuel tank. A total of 573 of the earlier turbojet- and turbofan-powered models was sold, including 215 -700s.

BRITISH AEROSPACE 125-800

Dimensions: Span, 51 ft 4½ in (15,66 m); length, 51 ft 2 in (15,59 m); height, 17 ft 7 in (5,37 m); wing area, 374 sq ft (32,75 m²).

BRITISH AEROSPACE 146-200

Country of Origin: United Kingdom.
Type: Short-haul regional airliner.
Power Plant: Four 6,968 lb st (3 160 kgp) Avco Lycoming ALF 502R-5 turbofans.
Performance: Max cruise speed, 483 mph (778 km/h) at 26,000 ft (7 925 m); econ cruise, 441 mph (710 km/h) at 30,000 ft (9 145 m); long-range cruise, 436 mph (702 km/h) at 30,000 ft (9 145 m); range (max payload), 1,232 mls (1 982 km) at econ cruise, (max fuel), 1,440 mls (2 317 km), or (with optional fuel capacity), 1,727 mls (2 780 km).
Weights: Operational empty, 48,500 lb (22 000 kg); max take-off, 89,500 lb (40 597 kg).
Accommodation: Flight crew of two and maximum seating (single-class) for 106 passengers six-abreast.
Status: First BAe 146-100 flown 3 September 1981, and first BAe 146-200 flown on 1 August 1982, with first customer deliveries of -100 (Dan Air) early 1983, and -200 (Air Wisconsin) March 1983. Forty-one BAe 146s ordered by beginning of 1985, plus 38 on option, and 25 aircraft flown.
Notes: The BAe 146 is currently being manufactured in -100 form with an 85 ft 10 in (26,16 m) fuselage for up to 82 passengers (illustrated above) and -200 form (described). The BAe 146 is optimised for operation over stage lengths of the order of 150 miles (240 km) with unrefuelled multi-stop capability. Apart from fuselage length and capacity, the two versions of the BAe 146 are similar in all respects, but the uprated R-5 version of the ALF 502 turbofan is available for the longer -200 model which is featured by most initial orders. The BAe 146-300, which is expected to fly in 1987, will feature a 10 ft 6 in (3,20 m) fuselage stretch to provide accommodation for 122–134 passengers.

BRITISH AEROSPACE 146-200

Dimensions: Span, 85 ft 5 in (26,34 m); length, 93 ft 8½ in (28,56 m); height, 28 ft 3 in (8,61 m); wing area, 832 sq ft (77,30 m²).

BRITISH AEROSPACE HAWK

Country of Origin: United Kingdom.
Type: Tandem two-seat basic/advanced trainer and light tactical aircraft.
Power Plant: One 5,200 lb st (2 360 kgp) Rolls-Royce Turboméca Adour 151, or (Srs 60) 5,700 lb st (2 585 kgp) Adour 861 turbofan.
Performance: (T Mk 1) Max speed (clean aircraft with one crew member) 622 mph (1 000 km/h) or Mach = 0·815 at sea level, 580 mph (933 km/h) or Mach = 0·88 at 36,000 ft (10 970 m); max climb, 11,833 ft/min (60,1 m/sec); tactical radius (with four 550-lb/250 kg bombs and two 130 Imp gal/590 l drop tanks), 680 mls (1 095 km) HI-LO-HI, 317 mls (510 km) LO-LO-LO.
Weights: Empty, 8,000 lb (3 629 kg); loaded (clean), 11,100 lb (5 040 kg); max take-off (ground attack), 18,390 lb (8 342 kg).
Armament: (Srs 100) Five external ordnance stations for max of 6,800 lb (3 100 kg) when flown as single-seater. Eighty-eight Hawk T Mk 1s were being modified at beginning of 1985 to carry two AIM-9 Sidewinder AAMs to provide secondary air defence capability as T Mk 1As.
Status: Pre-series Hawk flown 21 August 1974, with first of 175 for RAF flown 19 May 1975. Export versions include Mk 51 (Finland, 50), Mk 52 (Kenya, 12), Mk 53 (Indonesia, 20), Mk 60 (Zimbabwe, 8), Mk 61 (Dubai, 8), Mk 63 (Abu Dhabi, 16) and Mk 64 (Kuwait, 12). The T-45A is a carrier-capable development of the Hawk for the US Navy, scheduled to fly in December 1987. The T-45 is being developed jointly with McDonnell Douglas, the US Navy having a requirement for 309 T-45As. Currently on offer is the Series 100, which, similarly powered to the Series 60, has an inertial navigator, headup display, laser rangefinder and a weapon aiming computer. The single-seat Hawk 200 light strike fighter will fly in May 1986.

BRITISH AEROSPACE HAWK

Dimensions: Span, 30 ft 9¾ in (9,39 m); length, 38 ft 10⅔ in (11,85 m); height, 13 ft 1 in (4,00 m); wing area, 179·64 sq ft (16,69 m²).

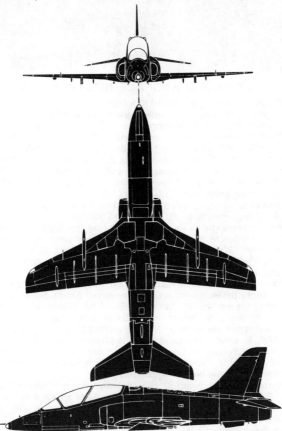

BRITISH AEROSPACE JETSTREAM 31

Country of Origin: United Kingdom.
Type: Light corporate transport and regional airliner.
Power Plant: Two 900 shp Garrett TPE 331-10 turboprops.
Performance: Max cruise speed, 299 mph (482 km/h) at 20,000 ft (6 100 m); long-range cruise, 265 mph (426 km/h) at 25,000 ft (7 620 m); initial climb, 2,200 ft/min (11,2 m/sec); max range (with 19 passengers and IFR reserves), 737 mls (1 186 km), (with 12 passengers), 1,094 mls (1 760 km), (with nine passengers), 1,324 mls (2 130 km).
Weights: Empty equipped (including flight crew), 8,840 lb (4 010 kg); max take-off, 14,550 lb (6 600 kg).
Accommodation: Two seats side by side on flight deck with basic corporate executive seating for eight passengers, with optional 12-seat executive shuttle arrangement, or up to 19 passengers three-abreast with offset aisle in high-density regional airline arrangement.
Status: First Jetstream 31 flown on 18 March 1982, following flight development aircraft (converted from a Series 1 airframe) flown on 28 March 1980. First customer delivery (Contactair of Stuttgart) made 15 December 1982. Jetstream 31 sales commitments totalled 69 aircraft by the beginning of 1985, in which year production is planned to attain a minimum of 25 aircraft. Some 24 aircraft were completed during the course of 1984 and 42 aircraft were in service with 11 operators by the beginning of 1985.
Notes: The Jetstream 31 is a derivative of the Handley Page H.P.137 Jetstream, the original prototype of which was flown on 18 August 1967. An inshore maritime patrol version, the Jetstream 31 EZ (Economic Zone) was under development at the beginning of 1984, this having 360-deg scan search radar.

BRITISH AEROSPACE JETSTREAM 31

Dimensions: Span, 52 ft 0 in (15,85 m); length, 47 ft 2 in (14,37 m); height, 17 ft 6 in (5,37 m); wing area, 270 sq ft (25,08 m²).

BRITISH AEROSPACE NIMROD AEW MK 3

Country of Origin: United Kingdom.
Type: Airborne warning and control system aircraft.
Power Plant: Four 12,160 lb st (5 515 kgp) Rolls-Royce RB.168-20 Spey Mk 250 turbofans.
Performance: No details have been released for publication, but maximum and transit speeds are likely to be generally similar to those of the MR Mk 2 (see 1984 edition), and maximum endurance is in excess of 10 hours. The mission requirement calls for 6–7 hours on station at 29,000-35,000 ft (8 840-10 670 m) at approx 350 mph (563 km/h) at 750-1,000 miles (1 120-1 600 km) from base.
Weights: Max take-off (approx), 190,000 lb (85 185 kg).
Accommodation: Flight crew of four and tactical team of six, latter comprising tactical air control officer, communications control officer, EWSM (Electronic Warfare Support Measures) operator and three air direction officers.
Status: Total of 11 Nimrod MR Mk 1 airframes have been rebuilt to AEW Mk 3 standard of which fully representative prototype flew on 16 July 1980. The Nimrod AEW Mk 3 is now expected to enter service with the RAF during 1986–87.
Notes: The Nimrod AEW Mk 3 is equipped with Marconi mission system avionics with identical radar aerials mounted in nose and tail, these being synchronised and each sequentially sweeping through 180 deg in azimuth in order to provide uninterrupted coverage throughout the 360 deg of combined sweep. EWSM pods are located at the wingtips and weather radar in the starboard wing pinion tank. The Nimrod AEW Mk 3 is intended to provide complementary capability with the Boeing E-3A Sentries operated by the NATO combined force (excluding the UK).

BRITISH AEROSPACE NIMROD AEW MK 3

Dimensions: Span, 115 ft 1 in (35,08 m); length, 137 ft 8½ in (41,97 m); height, 35 ft 0 in (10,67 m); wing area, 2,121 sq ft (197,05 m²).

BRITISH AEROSPACE SEA HARRIER

Country of Origin: United Kingdom.

Type: Single-seat V/STOL shipboard multi-role fighter.

Power Plant: One 21,500 lb st (9 760 kgp) Rolls-Royce Pegasus 104 vectored-thrust turbofan.

Performance: Max speed (clean aircraft), 720 mph (1 160 km/h) or Mach=0·95 at 1,000 ft (305 m), 607 mph (977 km/h) or Mach=0·92 at 36,000 ft (10 970 m), (with two AIM-9L AAMs and two Martel ASMs), 598 mph (962 km/h) or Mach=0·83 at sea level; combat radius (recce mission with two 100 Imp gal/455 l drop tanks), 518 mls (520 km); endurance (with two drop tanks for combat air patrol), 1·5 hrs at 115 mls/185 km from ship with three min combat.

Weights: Empty (approx), 13,000 lb (5 897 kg); normal loaded (STO), 21,700 lb (9 840 kg); max take-off 25,600 lb (11 612 kg).

Armament: Provision for two 30-mm cannon plus two AIM-9L Sidewinder AAMs and up to 5,000 lb (2 268 kg) ordnance on five external stations.

Status: First Sea Harrier (built on production tooling) flown on 20 August 1978, with deliveries against initial 34 ordered for Royal Navy completed during 1982 when follow-on batch of 14 aircraft ordered. Further nine ordered 1984 for 1986–88 delivery. Six (FRS Mk 51) ordered for Indian Navy with completion of deliveries early 1984.

Notes: The Royal Navy's Sea Harrier FRS Mk 1 is a derivative of the RAF's Harrier GR Mk 3 (see 1982 edition) to operate from *Invincible*-class through-deck cruisers. Changes for the naval role include a new forward fuselage with raised cockpit, nose installation of Blue Fox intercept radar, new operational equipment and various changes to airframe and engine to suit maritime environment. During 1984, contract awarded for a mid-life update involving installation of Blue Vixen pulse doppler radar. redesigned wing tips to provide two additional missile stations and provision for Hughes AIM-20 missiles.

BRITISH AEROSPACE SEA HARRIER

Dimensions: Span, 25 ft 3 in (7,70 m); length, 47 ft 7 in (14,50 m); height, 12 ft 2 in (3,70 m); wing area, 201·1 sq ft (18,68 m²).

CANADAIR CHALLENGER 601

Country of Origin: Canada.
Type: Light corporate transport.
Power Plant: Two 9,140 lb st (4 146 kgp) with 5-min limit or 8,650 lb st (3 924 kgp) General Electric CF34-1A turbofans.
Performance: Max cruising speed, 529 mph (851 km/h) or Mach = 0·8; normal cruise, 509 mph (819 km/h) or Mach = 0·77; range cruise, 488 mph (786 km/h) or Mach = 0·74; operational ceiling, 41,000 ft (12 500 m); range (max fuel and IFR reserves), 3,857 mls (6 208 km).
Weights: Empty, 19,950 lb (9 049 kg); operational empty (typical), 25,585 lb (11 605 kg); max take-off, 43,100 lb (19 550 kg).
Accommodation: Flight crew of two on flight deck wiith customer-specified main cabin interiors providing seating for up to 19 passengers.
Status: Prototype Challenger 601 flown on 10 April 1982, with FAA certification following on 25 February 1983. The 100th Challenger (including 81 Challenger 600s) delivered on 19 March 1984, and 33 Challenger 601s delivered by the beginning of 1985 when production was continuing at a rate of 1·5 monthly.
Notes: The Challenger 601 is the intercontinental-range derivative of the transcontinental Challenger 600, the latter differing primarily in having 7,500 lb st (3 402 kgp) Avco Lycoming ALF 502L turbofans. Production of this version was terminated mid-1983. Two Challengers have been procured by the Canadian Armed Forces and seven have been ordered by the *Luftwaffe*. Several versions of the Challenger were under study at the beginning of 1985, including cargo and AEW variants, and a winglet retrofit programme for the Challenger 600 was in progress.

CANADAIR CHALLENGER 601

Dimensions: Span, 64 ft 4 in (19,61 m); length, 68 ft 5 in (20,85 m); height, 20 ft 8 in (6,30 m) wing area (basic), 450 sq ft (41,82 m²).

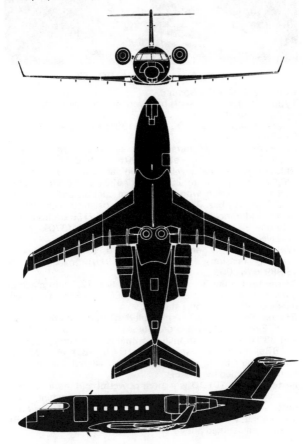

CASA C-101DD AVIOJET

Country of Origin: Spain.
Type: Tandem two-seat basic/advanced trainer and light tactical support aircraft.
Power Plant: One 4,700 lb st (2130 kgp) Garrett TFE-731-5 turbofan.
Performance: (Manufacturer's estimates) Max speed, 518 mph (834 km/h) at 15,000 ft (4570 m), 500 mph (805 km/h) at sea level; max initial climb, 5,300 ft/min (26,92 m/sec); time to 25,000 ft (7620 m), 7·5 min; tactical radius (interdiction with one 30-mm cannon and four 550-lb/250-kg bombs), 345 mls (556 km) LO-LO-LO with 10% reserves; endurance (armed patrol at 115 mls/185 km from base with one 30-mm cannon), 3·5 hrs at 230 mph (370 km/h) at sea level; max range, 2,300 mls (3700 km).
Weights: Empty equipped, 7,716 lb (3500 kg); loaded (training mission), 10,075 lb (4570 kg); max take-off, 13,889 lb (6300 kg).
Armament: One 30-mm cannon or two 12,7-mm machine guns in fuselage pod and up to 4,000 lb (1815 kg) of ordnance on six wing stores stations.
Status: The C-101DD is scheduled to enter flight test in May 1985. First of four Aviojet prototypes flown on 29 June 1977, and 88 (C-101EBs) supplied to Spanish Air Force, four (C-101BBs) to Honduras, and 17 (C-101BBs) and 20 (C-101CCs) are being supplied to Chile, all but the first five being assembled by ENAER.
Notes: The C-101DD is a more powerful and more comprehensively equipped (head-up display, weapon aiming computer, attitude and heading reference system, etc) version of the Aviojet with enhanced attack capability. The C-101BB version is illustrated above.

CASA C-101DD AVIOJET

Dimensions: Span, 34 ft 9⅜ in (10,60 m); length, 41 ft 0 in (12,50 m); height, 13 ft 11 in (4,25 m); wing area, 215·3 sq ft (20,00 m²).

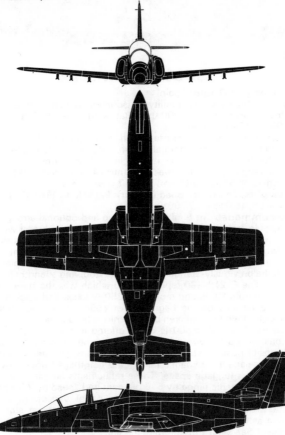

CASA C-212-300 AVIOCAR

Country of Origin: Spain.
Type: Military and civil utility transport and regional airliner.
Power Plant: Two 900 shp (flat-rated) Garrett TPE331-10R-512C turboprops.
Performance: Max cruise speed, 224 mph (360 km/h) at 25,000 ft (7 620 m); normal cruise, 225 mph (362 km/h) at 10,000 ft (3 050 m); max initial climb, 1,555 ft/min (7,9 m/sec); range (45 min reserves), 270 mls (435 km) with 28 passengers, 906 mls (1 458 km) with 17 passengers.
Weights: Empty equipped (freight), 9,072 lb (4 115 kg); max take-off, 16,975 lb (7 700 kg).
Accommodation: Flight crew of two and optional arrangements in main cabin for 26 or 28 passengers four abreast with central aisle, or 24 passengers three abreast with offset aisle.
Status: The C-212-300 version of the Aviocar was introduced in 1984 with (optional) an aerodynamic fairing replacing the previously-standard rear freight door and a lengthened nose. The C-212-300 replaces -200 which was the standard version from 1979, and more than 350 Aviocars (all versions) had been sold by the beginning of 1985 when production was also being undertaken by Nurtanio in Indonesia.
Notes: The C-212-300 is being offered in a variety of versions for both civil and military roles, the drawing on the opposite page illustrating the regional transport variant with rear fuselage aerodynamic fairing and lengthened nose providing extra luggage space. These refinements are claimed to increase specific range by 5–6 per cent and speed by 7.5 mph (12 km/h). An ASW and maritime patrol version of the C.212-300 features fuselage hardpoints for external stores such as the Sting Ray lightweight torpedo and the BAe Dynamics Sea Skua anti-shipping missile.

CASA C-212-300 AVIOCAR

Dimensions: Span, 62 ft 4 in (19,00 m); length, 49 ft 9 in (15,20 m); height, 20 ft 8 in (6,30 m); wing area, 430·56 sq ft (40,00 m²).

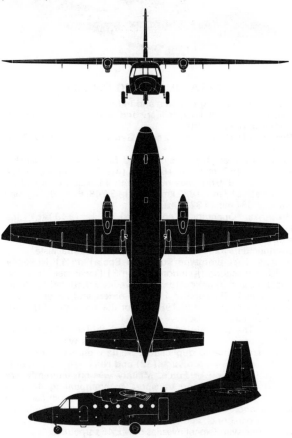

CASA-NURTANIO CN-235

Countries of Origin: Spain and Indonesia.
Type: Regional airliner, military and civil freighter and mixed personnel/freight transport.
Power plant: Two 1,772 eshp General Electric CT7-7 turboprops.
Performance: Max cruising speed (at 31,746 lb/14 400 kg), 281 mph (452 km/h) at 15,000 ft (4 570 m); service ceiling, 26,000 ft (7 925 m); max range (with 44 passengers and IFR reserves), 517 mls (832 km), (with 3,748-lb/1 700-kg payload), 2,684 mls (4 320 km).
Weights: Operational empty, 20,723 lb (9 400 kg); max take-off, 31,746 lb (14 400 kg).
Accommodation: Flight crew of two and standard seating arrangements for 44 or 40 passengers with central aisle.
Status: First prototype flown (in Spain) on 11 November 1983, and second (in Indonesia) on 31 December 1983. Certification and initial customer deliveries scheduled for fourth quarter of 1985. Total of 111 firm orders and 23 options recorded by beginning of 1985, 54 of the aircraft on firm order being military models.
Notes: The CN-235 is being built jointly by CASA of Spain and Nurtanio of Indonesia on a 50-50 basis without component manufacturing duplication. Military orders comprise 50 for the Indonesian Air Force (32) and Navy (18), and four for the Royal Saudi Air Force. Military versions currently proposed include a troop transport accommodating 41 paratroops, a freighter, an electronic warfare variant, an aeromedical transport accommodating 24 casualty stretchers and four medical personnel, and a maritime surveillance and ASW variant armed with Exocet missiles of Mk 46 torpedoes.

CASA-NURTANIO CN-235

Dimensions: Span, 84 ft 7⅝ in (25,81 m); length, 70 ft 0⅜ in (21,35 m); height, 26 ft 9¾ in (8·17 m); wing area, 636·17 sq ft (59,10 m²).

CESSNA 208 CARAVAN I

Country of Origin: USA.
Type: Light utility transport.
Power Plant: One 600 shp (flat-rated) Pratt & Whitney (Canada) PT6A-114 turboprop.
Performance: Max cruise speed, 214 mph (345 km/h) at 10,000 ft (3 050 m); max initial climb, 1,205 ft/min (6,12 m/sec); service ceiling, 30,000 ft (9 145 m); Range (max fuel and reserves), 1,139 mls (1 833 km).
Weights: Empty, 3,708 lb (1 682 kg); max take-off, 7,300 lb (3 311 kg).
Accommodation: Pilot and up to 13 passengers or equivalent freight. Passenger seating in combination of two and three abreast with aisle between seats.
Status: Engineering prototype flown on 9 December 1982, with first production aircraft being rolled out in August 1984, with first customer delivery (Federal Express) following in December. Production rate of six–eight monthly during 1985.
Notes: Claimed to be the first all-new single turboprop aircraft designed for the utility role to attain production status, the Caravan I bears little relationship to any previous Cessna design. Suitable for operation with skis and specially-designed Wipline floats, it is rapidly convertible from all-passenger to passenger-and-freight or all-freight configuration. The cabin can accommodate such loads as two D-size cargo containers or up to 10 fuel drums of 55 US (208 l) capacity. Federal Express has ordered 30 Caravan Is and taken an option on a further 70, and these differ from the standard configuration primarily in having passenger windows deleted and an underfuselage cargo pannier offset to port.

CESSNA 208 CARAVAN I

Dimensions: Span, 51 ft 10 in (15,80 m); length, 37 ft 7 in (11,45 m); height, 14 ft 2 in (4,29 m); wing area, 279·52 sq ft (25,97 m²).

CESSNA T-47A

Country of Origin: USA.

Type: Radar and navigational trainer.

Power Plant: Two 2,900 lb st (1 315 kgp) Pratt & Whitney (Canada) JT15D-5 turbofans.

Performance: Max speed, 484 mph (778 km/h) at 40,000 ft (12 190 m) or Mach = 0·733; cruise, 463 mph (746 km/h) at 35,000 ft (10 670 m); normal range, 2,110 mls (3 395 km).

Weights: Empty equipped, 9,035 lb (4 098 kg); max take-off, 15,000 lb (6 804 kg).

Accommodation: Crew comprises pilot, instructor and three students.

Status: First T-47A flown on 15 February 1984, and 15 ordered by US Navy for service from May 1985.

Notes: The T-47A is a derivative of the Citation S/II corporate transport (see 1984 edition) from which it differs principally in having more powerful engines and a shorter wing span. The T-47A is to be used by the US Navy in its Undergraduate Naval Flight Officer Training Systems Upgrade programme, training personnel in the use of air-to-air, air-to-surface, intercept and other radar equipment, operational procedures for navigation and airborne target acquisition. The aircraft have been procured under a five-year total training concept which includes the provision by Cessna of aircraft, pilots, simulators and maintenance services, plus a three-year option.

CESSNA T-47A

Dimensions: Span, 46 ft 6 in (14,18 m); length, 47 ft 10¾ in (14,60 m); height, 14 ft 9¾ in (4,51 m).

CESSNA 650 CITATION III

Country of Origin: USA.
Type: Light corporate transport.
Power Plant: Two 3,650 lb st (1 656 kgp) Garrett TFE731-3B-100S turbofans.
Performance: Max cruise speed (at 16,000 lb/7 258 kg), 544 mph (875 km/h) at 35,000 ft (10 670 m), 528 mph (850 km/h) at 41,000 ft (12 500 m); time to 35,000 ft (10 670 m) at 20,000 lb (9 072 kg), 14 min; range (with six passengers and 45 min reserve), 3,040 mls (4 894 km) at 482 mph (776 km/h) at 45,000 ft (13 715 m); ferry range, 3,200 mls (5 150 km).
Weights: Operational empty (average), 12,200 lb (5 534 kg); max take-off, 21,000 lb (9 526 kg).
Accommodation: Normal flight crew of two on flight deck and standard main cabin arrangement for six passengers in individual seats.
Status: Two prototypes flown on 30 May 1979 and 2 May 1980 respectively, with certification following on 30 April 1982, and customer deliveries commencing spring 1983. Fifty Citation IIIs were delivered during the course of 1984, the 41st aircraft having been the 1,200th Citation (of all types) produced by Cessna.
Notes: The Citation III owes nothing to preceding Citations despite its name, being of all new aerodynamic design and featuring a supercritical wing. The first production model established two time-to-altitude records in 1983 for aircraft in its class and a record by flying from Gander to Le Bourget in 5 hr 13 min.

CESSNA 650 CITATION III

Dimensions: Span, 53 ft 3½ in (16,30 m); length, 55 ft 6 in (16,90 m); height, 17 ft 3½ in (5,30 m); wing area, 312 sq ft (29,00 m²).

DASSAULT-BREGUET ATLANTIC G2 (ATL2)

Country of Origin: France.
Type: Long-range maritime patrol aircraft.
Power Plant: Two 5,665 shp Rolls-Royce/SNECMA Tyne RTy 20 Mk 21 turboprops.
Performance: Max speed, 368 mph (593 km/h) at sea level; normal cruise, 345 mph (556 km/h) at 25,000 ft (7 620 m); typical patrol speed, 196 mph (315 km/h); initial climb, 2,000 ft/min (10,1 m/sec); service ceiling, 30,000 ft (9 100 m); typical mission, 8 hrs patrol at 690 mls (1 110 km) from base at 2,000-3,000 ft (610-915 m); max range, 5,590 mls (9 000 km).
Weights: Empty equipped, 56,217 lb (25 500 kg); normal loaded weight, 97,885 lb (44 400 kg); max take-off, 101,850 lb (46 200 kg).
Accommodation: Normal flight crew of 12, comprising two pilots, flight engineer, forward observer, radio navigator, ESM/ECM/MAD operator, radar operator, tactical co-ordinator, two acoustic operators and two aft observers.
Armament: Up to eight Mk 46 homing torpedoes, nine 550-lb (250-kg) bombs or 12 depth charges, plus two AM 39 Exocet ASMs in forward weapons bay. Four wing stations with combined capacity of 7,715 lb (3 500 kg).
Status: First of two prototypes (converted from ATL1s) flown 8 May 1981, with second following on 26 March 1982, and series production authorised on 24 May 1984 with initial batch of 16 aircraft with deliveries to commence by 1989 against an *Aéronavale* requirement for 42 aircraft.
Notes: The Atlantic G2 (*Génération* 2), also referred to as the ATL2, is a modernised version of the Atlantic G1 (now referred to as the ATL1), production of which terminated in 1973 after completion of 87 series aircraft.

DASSAULT-BREGUET ATLANTIC G2 (ATL2)

Dimensions: Span, 122 ft 7 in (37,36 m); length, 107 ft 0$\frac{1}{4}$ in (36,62 m); height, 37 ft 1$\frac{1}{4}$ in (11,31 m); wing area, 1,295·3 sq ft (120,34 m²).

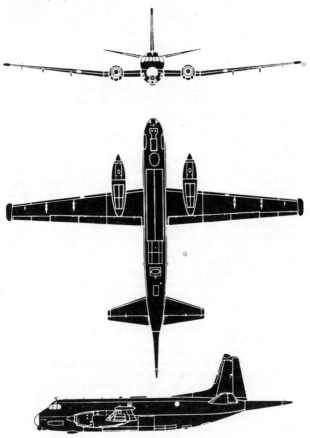

DASSAULT-BREGUET
MYSTERE-FALCON 900

Country of Origin: France.

Type: Light corporate transport.

Power Plant: Three 4,500 lb st (2 040 kgp) Garrett TFE 731-5A turbofans.

Performance: (Estimated) Max cruise, 554 mph (892 km/h) or Mach 0·84 at 39,000 ft (11 890 m); range cruise, 495 mph (797 km/h) or Mach=0·75 at 37,000 ft (11 275 m); range (with eight passengers at long-range cruise with IFR reserves), 4,375 mls (7 040 km), (with 19 passengers), 3,915 mls (6 300 km), (with max payload), 2,765 mls (4 450 km); max cruise altitude, 51,000 ft (15 550 m).

Weights: Operational empty, 23,400 lb (10 615 kg); max takeoff, 45,500 lb (20 640 kg).

Accommodation: Flight crew of two on flight deck and various arrangements in main cabin for 8–15 passengers. Optional arrangements for 19 passengers and provision included in basic design for additional emergency exits which will permit up to 34 passengers to be carried.

Status: First prototype flown on 21 September 1984, with second to follow in September 1985 and certification planned for March 1986.

Notes: The Mystère-Falcon 900 is a derivative of the Mystère-Falcon 50 (see 1982 edition) with which it shares some component commonality, but it features a longer, larger-diameter fuselage, longer span wing, higher-powered engines and various aerodynamic refinements. The Mystère-Falcon 900 possesses a larger cross-section cabin than the forthcoming Gulfstream IV and a longer cabin than the Canadair Challenger, its principal competitors.

DASSAULT-BREGUET MYSTERE-FALCON 900

Dimensions: Span, 63 ft 5 in (19,33 m); length, 66 ft 5$\frac{1}{4}$ in (20,25 m); height, 24 ft 9$\frac{1}{4}$ in (7,55 m); wing area, 527·77 sq ft (49,03 m²).

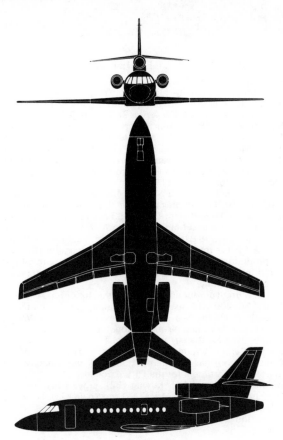

DASSAULT-BREGUET MIRAGE F1

Country of Origin: France.

Type: Single-seat multi-role fighter.

Power Plant: One 11,023 lb st (5 000 kgp) dry and 15,873 lb st (7 200 kgp) reheat SNECMA Atar 9K50 turbojet.

Performance: (F1C) Max speed (clean aircraft), 914 mph (1 470 km/h) or Mach = 1·2 at sea level, 1,450 mph (2 555 km/h) or Mach = 2·2 at 39,370 ft (12 000 m); initial climb, 41,930 ft/min (213 m/sec); service ceiling, 65,600 ft (20 000 m); tactical radius (with two drop tanks and 4,410 lb/ 2 000 kg bombs), 670 mls (1 078 km).

Weights: Empty, 16,314 lb (7 400 kg); normal loaded, 24,030 lb (10 900 kg); max take-off, 32,850 lb (14 900 kg).

Armament: Two 30-mm DEFA 553 cannon and (intercept) one-three Matra 550 Magic plus two AIM-9 AAMs, or (close support) up to 8,818 lb (4 000 kg) of external ordnance.

Status: First of four prototypes flown 23 December 1966, and first production aircraft flown 15 February 1973, with 643 delivered by beginning of 1985 and production continuing at a rate of 2·5 monthly.

Notes: Current production models for the *Armée de l'Air* consist of the F1C-200 with fixed flight refuelling probe, the tactical recce F1CR and the two-seat F1B conversion trainer. Whereas the F1C is a dedicated air-air version, the export F1A and F1E are optimised for the air-ground role. The two-seat model retains the Cyrano IV radar, weapon system and missile capability of the F1C, but has no internal guns and fuel capacity is reduced. Foreign orders for the F1 are Ecuador (18), Iraq (89), Jordan (36), Qatar (14), Kuwait (32), Libya (38), Morocco (50), Greece (40), South Africa (48) and Spain (73). The *Armée de l'Air* is receiving 227 Mirage F1s, comprising 164 F1Cs, 43 F1CRs and 20 F1Bs with deliveries to be completed during 1985.

DASSAULT-BREGUET MIRAGE F1

Dimensions: Span, 27 ft 6¾ in (8,40 m); length, 49 ft 2½ in (15,00 m); height, 14 ft 9 in (4,50 m); wing area, 269·1 sq ft (25,00 m²).

DASSAULT-BREGUET MIRAGE 2000N

Country of Origin: France.
Type: Tandem two-seat low-altitude attack fighter.
Power Plant: One 14,460 lb st (6 560 kgp) dry and 21,385 lb st (9 700 kgp) reheat SNECMA M53-P2 turbofan.
Performance: Max speed (clean aircraft), 915 mph (1 472 km/h) at sea level or Mach=1.2, 1,550 mph (2 495 km/h) or Mach=2·35 (short endurance dash) above 36,090 ft (11 000 m); typical penetration speed (with ASMP), 690 mph (1 110 km/h) or Mach=0·905 at 200 ft (60 m); approx tactical radius LO-LO-LO (with ASMP annd external fuel), 300 mls (483 km).
Weights: Max take-off, 33,070 lb (15 000 kg).
Armament: One ramjet-powered nuclear Aérospatiale ASMP (*Air-Sol Moyenne Portée*) stand-off missile or up to 13,227 lb (6 000 kg) of ordnance distributed between nine external stations.
Status: First and second prototypes of Mirage 2000N (*Nucléaire*) penetration aircraft flown on 3 February and 21 September 1983, and 47 funded (1983–85) from planned *Armée de l'Air* total of 85 aircraft, with 36 to be delivered by end of 1988.
Notes: The Mirage 2000N is a two-seat low-altitude penetration version of the Mirage 2000C (see 1984 edition) single-seat interceptor and air superiority fighter. For its specialised role it has EMD/Thomson-CSF Antilope 5 terrain-following radar and two intertial platforms, and in *Armée de l'Air* service its primary weapon will be the 100–150 Kt ASMP with a 46–62 mile (75–100 km) range intended for use against heavily-defended targets. Deliveries of the Mirage 2000N are scheduled to commence in 1986.

DASSAULT-BREGUET MIRAGE 2000N

Dimensions: Span, 29 ft 6 in (9,00 m); length, 47 ft 9 in (14,55 m); wing area, 441·3 sq ft (41,00 m²).

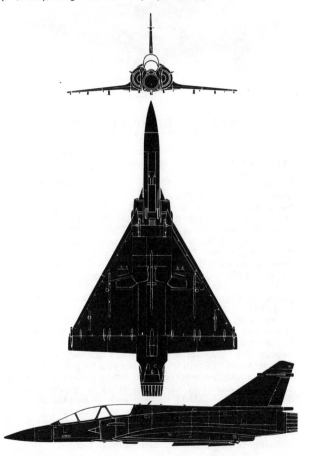

DASSAULT-BREGUET/DORNIER
ALPHA JET NGEA

Countries of Origin: France and Federal Germany.
Type: Tandem two-seat advanced trainer and light tactical support aircraft.
Power Plant: Two 3,175 lb st (1 440 kgp) SNECMA/Turboméca Larzac 04-C20 turbofans.
Performance: Max speed (clean), 572 mph (920 km/h) or Mach = 0·86 at 32,800 ft (10 000 m), 645 mph (1 038 km/h) at sea level; max initial climb, 11,220 ft/min (57 m/sec); service ceiling, 48,000 ft (14 630 m); tactical radius (LO-LO-LO with gun pod, two 137·5 Imp gal/625 l drop tanks and underwing ordnance), 391 mls (630 km), (without drop tanks), 242 mls (390 km), (HI-LO-HI with drop tanks), 668 mls (1 075 km), (without drop tanks), 363 mls (583 km).
Weights: Empty equipped, 7,749 lb (3 515 kg); max take-off, 17,637 lb (8 000 kg).
Armament: (Tactical air support) Max of 5,510 lb (2 500 kg) of external ordnance distributed between one fuselage and four wing stations.
Status: The Alpha Jet NGEA entered flight test in April 1982. Four delivered to Egypt in following year by parent company, and co-production with Egyptian industry continuing at rate of two per month at beginning of 1985 against Egyptian orders for 30 of (MS1) training and 15 of (MS 2) attack versions. Six of MS2 version ordered by Cameroun.
Notes: The Alpha Jet NGEA (*Nouvelle Génération Ecole-Appui*) is an improved attack version of the basic aircraft with a nav/attack system and uprated engines.

DASSAULT-BREGUET/DORNIER ALPHA JET NGEA

Dimensions: Span, 29 ft 11 in (9,11 m); length, 40 ft 3 in (12,29 m); height, 13 ft 9 in (4,19 m); wing area, 188 sq ft (17,50 m²).

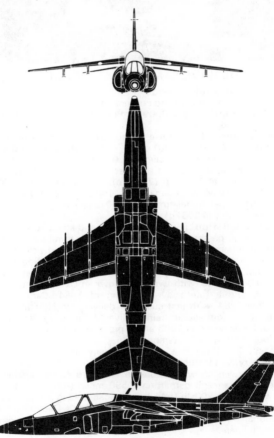

DE HAVILLAND CANADA DASH 8

Country of Origin: Canada.

Type: Regional airliner and corporate transport.

Power Plant: Two 2,000 shp Pratt & Whitney (Canada) PW120 turboprops.

Performance: Max cruise speed, 311 mph (500 km/h) at 15,000 ft (4 570 m), 301 mph (484 km/h) at 25,000 ft (7 620 m); max initial climb, 2,070 ft/min (10,51 m/sec); range (36 passengers and IFR reserves), 691 mls (1 112 km) at max cruise at 25,000 ft (7 620 m); max range (with 4,550-lb/2 064-kg payload and max fuel), 1,493 mls (2 402 km).

Weights: Operational empty, 21,590 lb (9 793 kg); max take-off, 33,000 lb (14 968 kg).

Accommodation: Flight crew of two and standard arrangement for 36 passengers four-abreast with central aisle. Alternate arrangements for 38–39 passengers, mixed passenger-cargo operations and corporate executive transportation.

Status: The first of four pre-production prototypes was flown on 20 June 1983, with two more flown in October and November, and a fourth by beginning of 1984. Certification October 1984, with first customer delivery (to NorOntair) in that month, four aircraft being delivered during the year, with 33 to be delivered in 1985 and a projected production tempo of four monthly by September 1985.

Notes: The Dash 8 is an evolutionary design embodying service-proven features of the Dash 7 (see 1984 edition). The corporate version will feature an extended range capability, additional tankage permitting 2,590 miles (4 167 km) to be flown with a 1,200-lb (544-kg) payload at long-range cruise. Six Dash 8Ms ordered in 1984 by Canada's Department of National Defence, four of these being equipped as navigational trainers.

DE HAVILLAND CANADA DASH 8

Dimensions: Span, 85 ft 0 in (25,91 m); length, 73 ft 0 in (22,25 m); height, 25 ft 0 in (7,62 m); wing area, 585 sq ft (54,35 m²).

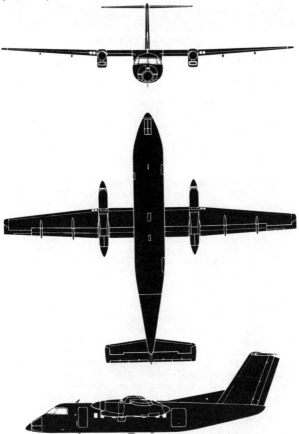

DORNIER DO 228

Country of Origin: Federal Germany.

Type: Light regional airliner and utility transport.

Power Plant: Two 715 shp Garrett AiResearch TPE 331-5 turboprops.

Performance: Max cruise speed, 268 mph (432 km/h) at 10,000 ft (3 280 m), 230 mph (370 km/h) at sea level; initial climb, 2,050 ft/min (10,4 m/sec); service ceiling, 29,600 ft (9 020 m); range (-100), 1,224 mls (1 970 km) at max range cruise, 1,075 mls (1 730 km) at max cruise, (-200), 715 mls (1 150 km) at max range cruise, 640 mls (1 030 km) at max cruise.

Weights: Operational empty (-100), 7,132 lb (3 235 kg), (-200), 7,450 lb (3 379 kg); max take-off, 12,570 lb (5 700 kg).

Accommodation: Flight crew of two and standard arrangements for (-100) 15 and (-200) 19 passengers in individual seats with central aisle.

Status: Prototype Do 228-100 flown on 28 March and -200 on 9 May 1981, and first customer delivery (A/S Norving) August 1982. Approximately 70 Do 228s (both -100s and -200s) ordered by beginning of 1985 (plus some 40 on option), in which year production is scheduled to rise from three to four aircraft monthly.

Notes: The Do 228 mates a new-technology wing of super-critical section with the fuselage cross-section of the Do 128 (see 1982 edition), and two versions differing essentially in fuselage length and range capability are currently in production, the shorter-fuselage Do 228-100 and the longer-fuselage Do 228-200 (illustrated on opposite page). All-cargo and corporate transport versions of the -100 are being offered. The -101 and -201 versions offer increased take-off weights. The Do 228 has been selected by India to meet that country's LTA (Light Transport Aircraft) requirement. Ten are to be supplied by Dornier with approximately 140 to be built in India by HAL over a 10-year period.

DORNIER DO 228

Dimensions: Span, 55 ft 7 in (16,97 m); length (-100) 49 ft 3 in (15,03 m), (-200), 54 ft 3 in (16,55 m); height, 15 ft 9 in (4,86 m); wing area, 344·46 sq ft (32,00 m²).

(CLAUDIUS) DORNIER SEASTAR

Country of Origin: Federal Germany.
Type: Light utility amphibious flying boat.
Power Plant: Two 500 shp Pratt & Whitney (Canada) PT6A-11 turboprops.
Performance: (Estimated) Max speed, 255 mph (410 km/h) at 6,560 ft (2 000 m); normal cruise, 200 mph (324 km/h) at 9,840 ft (3 000 m); initial climb (at 8,377 lb/3 800 kg), 1,770 ft/min (9,0 m/sec); range (with 3,000-lb/1 360-kg payload), 250 mls (402 km), (with 2,000-lb/907-kg payload), 545 mls (877 km).
Weights: Empty, 4,515 lb (2 048 kg); max take-off, 8,855 lb (4 017 kg).
Accommodation: Pilot and co-pilot/passenger side-by-side on flight deck and various arrangements for up to eight passengers in main cabin.
Status: The first prototype Seastar was flown on 17 August 1984, and current planning envisages certification by the end of 1986, with full-scale production commencing in the following year.
Notes: The Seastar has been developed by a team led by Prof Dipl-Ing Claudius Dornier (the project having no connection with Dornier GmbH) with the aim of meeting a requirement for a versatile light utility amphibian. Utilising glassfibre and carbonfibre composite construction to result in a corrosion-resistant hull, the Seastar is of centreline thrust concept with tandem-mounted engines and features a high-lift wing with fixed leading-edge slots and large-area trailing-edge flaps to achieve STOL capability. The Seastar will be capable of operation from grass, water, snow and ice, and will have a large upward-hinging freight loading door in the aft portside.

(CLAUDIUS) DORNIER SEASTAR

Dimensions: Span, 48 ft 6⅔ in (14,80 m); length, 36 ft 5 in (11,10 m); height, 14 ft 5¼ in (4,40 m); wing area, 258·34 sq ft (24,00 m²).

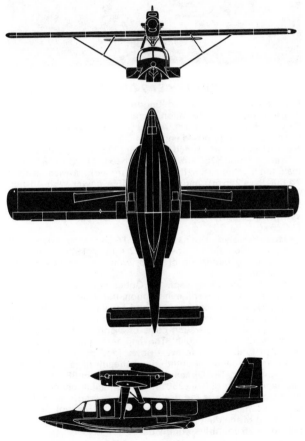

EDGLEY EA7 OPTICA

Country of Origin: United Kingdom.
Type: Three-seat observation aircraft.
Power Plant: One 260 hp Avco Lycoming IO-540 six-cylinder horizontally-opposed engine.
Performance: Max speed, 132 mph (213 km/h); cruise (55% power), 97 mph (156 km/h); loiter speed, 61 mph (98 km/h); max initial climb, 800 ft/min (4,06 m/sec); service ceiling, 14,000 ft (4 265 m); endurance (at 55% power with 45 min reserves), 5·5 hrs, (at loiter speed), 6·5 hrs; range (max fuel), 540 mls (869 km).
Weights: Empty, 1,875 lb (850 kg); max take-off, 2,725 lb (1 236 kg).
Status: Prototype Optica flown on 14 December 1979, with first production aircraft flown on 22 August 1984. Orders for 80 aircraft by beginning of 1985, with production rising to five per month by mid-year.
Notes: Of unique concept, the Optica is intended primarily for pipeline and powerline inspection, traffic surveillance, forestry, coastal and frontier patrol, and aerial photography, tasks that it is claimed capable of performing at less than one-third of the initial and operating costs of a comparable helicopter normally utilised for such. The engine is part of a ducted propulsor unit which forms a power pod separate from the main shroud and mounted downstream of a five-bladed fixed-pitch fan. The Optica can take-off within 980 ft (300 m) and land within 820 ft (250 m). The principal change in the production Optica is the use of a more powerful IO-540 engine, this having involved redesign of the central pod and reshaping of the duct profile. Orders for the Optica have been placed by 25 countries worldwide.

EDGLEY EA7 OPTICA

Dimensions: Span, 39 ft 4 in (12,00 m); length, 26 ft 9 in (8,15 m); height, 7 ft 7 in (2,31 m); wing area, 170·5 sq ft (15,84 m²).

EMBRAER EMB-120 BRASILIA

Country of Origin: Brazil.
Type: Short-haul regional airliner.
Power Plant: Two 1,500 shp Pratt & Whitney (Canada) PW115 turboprops.
Performance: (At max take-off weight) Max speed, 359 mph (578 km/h) at 20,000 ft (6 100 m); max cruise, 345 mph (555 km/h) at 20,000 ft (6 100 m); long-range cruise, 303 mph (487 km/h); max initial climb, 2,320 ft/min (11,78 m/sec); service ceiling, 29,500 ft (8 990 m); range (30 passengers and reserves), 691 mls (1 112 km); max range (max fuel and 14 passengers), 1,957 mls (3 150 km).
Weights: Empty equipped (standard), 14,240 lb (6 459 kg); max take-off, 23,810 lb (10 800 kg).
Accommodation: Flight crew of two and optional arrangements for 24, 26 and 30 passengers three abreast with offset aisle.
Status: First, second and third prototypes flown on 27 July and 21 December 1983, and 9 May 1984 respectively. Twenty-seven orders and 86 deposits recorded by beginning of 1985, with 12 to be produced during year, rising to 20 in 1986 and 25 per year thereafter.
Notes: A corporate executive transport version of the Brasilia was under active development at the beginning of 1985, together with several military versions. The Brazilian Air Force has a requirement for 24 Brasilias for transport tasks, and maritime surveillance and airborne early warning versions are currently under development.

EMBRAER EMB-120 BRASILIA

Dimensions: Span, 64 ft 10¾ in (19,78 m); length, 65 ft 7 in (20,00 m); height, 20 ft 10 in (6,35 m); wing area, 424·42 sq ft (39,43 m²).

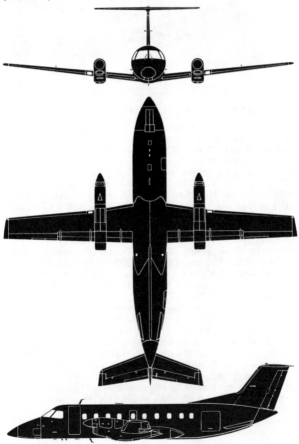

EMBRAER EMB-312 (T-27) TUCANO

Country of Origin: Brazil.

Type: Tandem two-seat basic trainer.

Power Plant: One 750 shp Pratt & Whitney (Canada) PT6A-25C turboprop.

Performance: (At max clean weight) Max speed, 269 mph (433 km/h) at 10,000 ft (3 050 m); max cruise, 255 mph (411 km/h) at 10,000 ft (3 050 m); econ cruise, 198 mph (319 km/h); max initial climb, 2,180 ft/min (11,07 m/sec); service ceiling 24,000 ft (7 315 m); range (max internal fuel with 30 min reserves), 1,145 mls (1 844 km); ferry range (two 145 Imp gal/660 l ferry tanks), 2,069 mls (3 330 km).

Weights: Basic empty, 3,991 lb (1 810 kg); loaded (clean) 5,622 lb (2 550 kg); max take-off, 7,000 lb (3 175 kg).

Armament: (Weapons training and light strike) Four wing hardpoints each stressed for 551 lb (250 kg). Max external ordnance load of 2,205 lb (1 000 kg).

Status: First of four prototypes flown on 15 August 1980, with production deliveries following from 29 September 1983 against Brazilian Air Force order for 118 (plus option on a further 50). One hundred and twenty (with options on further 60) ordered by Egypt (80 plus 20 on option for Iraq) of which 10 supplied in flyaway condition and remainder assembled from kits with progressive participation in component manufacture. Twelve ordered by Honduras. Approximately 100 delivered by beginning of 1985 when production was five–six monthly.

Notes: The Tucano (Toucan) was winner of the RAF's AST 412 requirement at beginning of 1985.

EMBRAER EMB-312 (T-27) TUCANO

Dimensions: Span, 36 ft 6½ in (11,14 m); length, 32 ft 4¼ in (9,86 m); height, 11 ft 1⅞ in (3,40 m); wing area, 208·82 sq ft (19,40 m²).

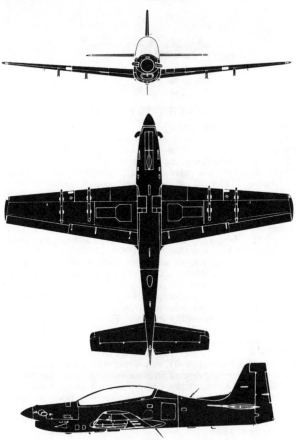

ENAER T-35 PILLAN

Country of Origin: Chile.
Type: Tandem two-seat primary/basic trainer.
Power Plant: One 300 hp Avco Lycoming AEIO-540-H1K5 six-cylinder horizontally-opposed engine.
Performance: (At max take-off weight) Max speed, 193 mph (311 km/h) at sea level; cruise (75% power), 185 mph (298 km/h) at 8,000 ft (2 680 m), (55% power), 159 mph (255 km/h) at 16,800 ft (5 120 m); initial climb, 1,516 ft/min (7,7 m/sec); service ceiling, 19,100 ft (5 822 m); range (45 min reserves at 75% power), 679 mls (1 093 km).
Weights: Empty, 1,836 lb (832 kg); empty equipped, 2,048 lb (929 kg); max take-off, 2,900 lb (1 315 kg).
Armament: (Light strike and armament training) Two pods of four or seven rockets, 250-lb (113,4-kg) bombs or 12,7-mm machine gun pods.
Status: First of two prototypes assembled by Piper flown on 6 March 1981, three additional aircraft being supplied by Piper as kits for assembly in Chile. First production aircraft against Chilean Air Force requirement for 80 rolled out by ENAER on 7 March 1984. Forty ordered by Spanish Air Force (by which named Tamiz). First delivery December 1984.
Notes: The Pillán (Devil) was designed under contract by Piper's Lakeland Advanced Engineering and Experimental Department and utilises some components of earlier Piper light aircraft (Cherokee series). Manufacture has been progressively transferred to ENAER (Empresa Nacional de Aéronautica de Chile) and about a dozen Pilláns had been delivered by the beginning of 1985.

ENAER T-35 PILLAN

Dimensions: Span, 28 ft 11 in (8,81 m); length, 26 ft 1 in (7,97 m); height, 7 ft 8⅛ in (7,70 m); wing area, 147 sq ft (13,64 m²).

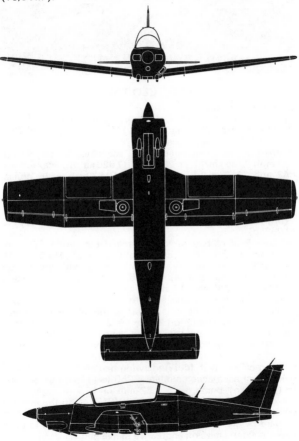

FAIRCHILD T-46A

Country of Origin: USA.

Type: Side-by-side two-seat primary/basic trainer.

Power Plant: Two 1,330 lb st (603 kgp) Garrett F109-GA-100 (TFE76-4A) turbofans.

Performance: (Manufacturer's estimates) Max speed, 457 mph (736 km/h) at 25,000 ft (7 620 km/h); max cruise, 442 mph (712 km/h) at 35,000 ft (10 670 m); econ cruise, 383 mph (616 km/h) at 45,000 ft (13 720 m); max initial climb, 4,470 ft/min (22,7 m/sec); service ceiling, 46,500 ft (14 175 m); ferry range, 1,324 mls (2 130 km).

Weights: Empty, 5,184 lb (2 351 kg); max take-off, 6,817 lb (3 092kg).

Status: First of two prototypes rolled out on 11 February 1985 and scheduled to enter flight test April 1985. USAF requirement through 1992 for 650 aircraft, with production deliveries commencing April 1986, with production peaking in 1990 and 1991 with 12 aircraft monthly.

Notes: Intended as a successor to the Cessna T-37 in USAF service, the T-46A was selected as winner of a new-generation trainer competition on 2 July 1982. Fairchild is developing from the basic pilot trainer an armed version as the AT-46A. This private venture derivative will be suitable for armament training, forward air control and light attack duties, and is being offered with four underwing hardpoints. The inboard pylons will each accommodate a 250-lb (113,4-kg) or 500-lb (226,8-kg) bomb, or a 7,62-mm or 12,7-mm gun pod, maximum station loads being 700 lb (317 kg) on the inboard pylons and 300 lb (136 kg) on the outboard pylons. The two inboard pylons will be plumbed for 56 Imp gal (254 l) drop tanks to extend mission endurance to five hours.

FAIRCHILD T-46A

Dimensions: Span, 38 ft 7¾ in (11,78 m); length, 29 ft 6 in (8,99 m); height, 12 ft 8 in (3,86 m); wing area, 160·9 sq ft (14,95 m²).

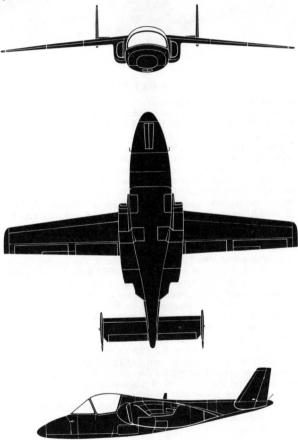

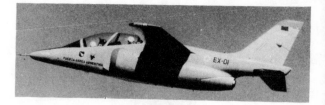

FMA IA 63 PAMPA

Country of Origin: Argentina.

Type: Tandem two-seat basic and advanced trainer.

Power Plant: One 3,500 lb st (1 588 kgp) Garrett TFE731-2N turbofan.

Performance: (Manufacturer's estimates at 7,055 lb/3,200 kg) Max speed, 460 mph (740 km/h) at sea level; initial climb 5,315 ft/min (27 m/sec); service ceiling, 42,325 ft (12 900 m); range (max internal fuel), 930 mls (1 500 km) at 345 mph (560 km/h) at 13,125 ft (4 000 m).

Weights: Normal loaded (flying training mission), 7,716 lb (3 500 kg); max take-off (armament training and light attack), 10,250 lb (4 500 kg).

Status: First of three flying prototypes flown on 6 October 1984, with second and third prototypes scheduled to follow in February and May 1985. The first batch of 12 aircraft to be delivered to Argentine Air Force late 1987 against anticipated initial order for 64 aircraft, operational status being attained in March 1988, peak production rate being three per month.

Notes: The Pampa, developed by the Dornier concern of Federal Germany under contract to the FMA (Fabrica Militar de Aviones), will enter service with the Argentine *Escuela de Aviación Militar* in March 1988. It is anticipated that an optimised light strike version of the Pampa will be developed with a 4,300 lb st (1 950 kgp) Garrett TFE731-5 engine—the basic version has inbuilt provision for up to five external stores stations—and that some 36 of the Argentine Air Force's total requirement of some 100 aircraft will be completed in this model for operational service from 1990–91. The Dornier concern is now acting only in an advisory capacity in the Pampa programme.

FMA IA 63 PAMPA

Dimensions: Span, 31 ft 9½ in (9,69 m); length, 35 ft 10¼ in (10,93 m); height, 14 ft 0¾ in (4,29 m); wing area, 168·24 sq ft (15,63 m²).

FOKKER F27 MARITIME ENFORCER

Country of Origin: Netherlands.
Type: Maritime surveillance, anti-submarine and anti-shipping aircraft.
Power Plant: Two 2,410 ehp Rolls-Royce Dart 552 turboprops.
Performance: Max speed, 295 mph (474 km/h) at 20,000 ft (6 100 m); cruise (at 38,000 lb/17 237 kg), 287 mph (463 km/h) at 20,000 ft (6 100 m); typical search speed, 167–201 mph (269–324 km/h) at 2,000 ft (610 m); service ceiling, 25,000 ft (7 620 m); max range (with five per cent and 30-min reserves), 3,107 mls (5 000 km) at 23,000–25,000 ft (7 010–7 620 m); mission endurance (SAR), 9·4 hrs, (ASW with 49 sonobuoys and four torpedoes), 7·8 hrs.
Weights: Operational empty, 30,260 lb (13 726 kg); normal loaded, 45,000 lb (20 410 kg); max take-off (emergency), 50,000 lb (22 680 kg).
Armament: External strong points comprise three under each wing and one on each side of fuselage. A pair of anti-shipping missiles (AM 39 Exocet, BAe Sea Eagle or AGM-84A Harpoon) can be carried on the fuselage points, maximum ordnance load comprising four torpedoes on wing points.
Status: Maritime Enforcer derived in 1984 from MPA Maritime (of which 16 sold to Peru, Spain, the Netherlands, Angola, the Philippines and Thailand). Deliveries can be made before the end of 1986.
Notes: The Maritime Enforcer is one of a number of military derivatives of the F27 Mk 200 Friendship airliner, 759 (all versions) of which had been sold by the beginning of 1985 (including 205 built by Fairchild). Other versions include the basic unarmed Maritime, the Sentinel for border surveillance and the proposed Kingbird airborne early warning variant.

FOKKER F27 MARITIME ENFORCER

Dimensions: Span, 95 ft 1¾ in (29,00 m); length, 77 ft 3½ in (23,55 m); height, 28 ft 6¾ in (8,70 m); wing area, 754 sq ft (70,00 m²).

FOKKER F28 FELLOWSHIP MK 4000

Country of Origin: Netherlands.

Type: Short/medium-haul commercial airliner.

Power Plant: Two 9,850 lb st (4 468 kgp) Rolls-Royce RB. 183-2 Spey Mk 555-15H turbofans.

Performance: Max cruising speed, 523 mph (843 km/h) at 23,000 ft (7 000 m); econ cruise, 487 mph (783 km/h) at 32,000 ft (9 755 m); range cruise, 421 mph (678 km/h) at 30,000 ft (9 145 m); range (with max payload), 1,160 mls (1 870 km), (with max fuel), 2,566 mls (4 130 km); cruise altitude, 35,000 ft (10 675 m).

Weights: Operational empty, 38,825 lb (17 661 kg); max take-off, 73,000 lb (33 110 kg).

Accommodation: Flight crew of two (with jump seat for optional third crew member) and basic main cabin single-class configuration for 85 passengers five-abreast.

Status: First of two F28 prototypes flown on 8 May 1967, with first customer delivery following on 24 February 1969. Total of 216 ordered by beginning of 1985 and production running at one monthly.

Notes: The F28 Mk 4000, which first flew in October 1976, provides the bulk of current production, the Mks 3000 and 4000 having supplanted the Mks 1000 and 2000 (after completion of 97 and 10 respectively). Whereas the Mk 3000 has the 80 ft 6½ in (24,55 m) fuselage of the Mk 1000, offering seating for up to 65 passengers, the Mk 4000 has the lengthened fuselage introduced by the Mk 2000. Work was proceeding at the beginning of 1985 on a follow-on development, the Fokker 100 with Rolls-Royce Tay turbofans, a lengthened fuselage and extended, redesigned wings. To fly mid-1986, the Fokker 100 has been ordered by Swissair.

FOKKER F28 FELLOWSHIP MK 4000

Dimensions: Span, 82 ft 3 in (25,07 m); length, 97 ft 1¾ in (29,61 m); height, 27 ft 9½ in (8,47 m); wing area, 850 sq ft (78,97 m²).

FOKKER 50

Country of Origin: Netherlands.

Type: Short-haul commercial airliner.

Power Plant: Two 2,150 shp Pratt & Whitney (Canada) PW124 turboprops.

Performance: (Manufacturer's estimates) Typical cruise speed, 330 mph (532 km/h); max operational altitude, 25,000 ft (7 620 m); range (at 41,888 lb/19 000 kg), 829 mls (1 334 km), (at 45,900 lb/20 820 kg), 1,739 mls (2 798 km).

Weights: Typical operational empty, 27,300 lb (12 383 kg); max take-off (standard), 41,888 lb (19 000kg), (optional), 45,900 lb (20 820 kg).

Accommodation: Crew of two on flight deck plus two cabin attendants and alternative layouts for 46 (business class), 54, 58 or 60 pasengers in four-abreast seating with central aisle.

Status: The first Fokker 50 is scheduled to enter flight test in November 1985. Certification is planned for July 1986, with customer deliveries following in 1987, 10 (plus five on option) having been ordered by Ansett and six (with six on option) by DLT.

Notes: A follow-on development of the F27 Friendship, the Fokker 50 is based on the proven airframe of the earlier airliner with significant structural and detail changes, allied to more fuel-efficient engines and increased use of composite materials. Differences from the current F27 include new-technology engines in redesigned nacelles and driving six-bladed propellers, use of carbon, aramid and glassfibre components in such areas as the wings, tailplane, fin and engine nacelles. More windows have been provided in the passenger cabin and the passenger door has been relocated.

FOKKER 50

Dimensions: Span, 95 ft 1¾ in (29,00 m); length, 82 ft 7¾ in (25,19 m); height, 28 ft 2½ in (8,60 m); wing area, 753·5 sq ft (70,00 m²).

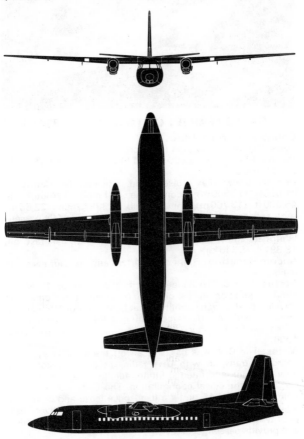

GATES LEARJET C-21A (LEARJET 35A)

Country of Origin: USA.

Type: Operational support transport.

Power Plant: Two 3,500 lb st (1 588 kgp) Garrett TFE731-2-2B turbofans.

Performance: Max cruise speed, 534 mph (860 km/h) at 41,000 ft (12 500 m); econ cruise, 481 mph (774 km/h) at 45,000 ft (13 700 m); initial climb, 4,339 ft/min (22,05 m/sec); service ceiling, 45,000 ft (13 715 m); range (six passengers and 45 min reserves), 2,423 mls (3 900 km).

Weights: Empty equipped, 9,924 lb (4 500 kg); max take-off, 18,397 lb (8 345 kg).

Accommodation: Flight crew of two and six–eight seats in main cabin.

Status: First C-21A handed over to the USAF on 13 March 1984. Production against order for 80 aircraft (plus option on 20 additional aircraft) continuing at beginning of 1985 at four monthly with 40 delivered during 1984 and completion scheduled for October 1985, or (if option taken up) March 1986.

Notes: The C-21A is basically an off-the-shelf Learjet 35A corporate transport with UHF radio, Tacan, provision for a ferry fuel tank and internal fittings for quick conversion to a cargo or aeromedical configuration. The C-21A is being acquired by the USAF under a fixed-price lease and contractor logistic support contract, its mission being "to deliver high-priority and time-sensitive freight, season newly-rated pilots and provide passenger airlift".

GATES LEARJET C-21A (LEARJET 35A)

Dimensions: Span, 39 ft 6 in (12,04 m); length, 48 ft 8 in (14,83 m); height, 12 ft 3 in (3,73 m); wing area, 253·3 sq ft (23,53 m²).

GATES-PIAGGIO GP-180

Countries of Origin: USA and Italy.

Type: Light corporate transport.

Power Plant: Two 800 shp Pratt & Whitney (Canada) PT6A-66 turboprops.

Performance: (Manufacturer's estimates) Max speed, 460 mph (740 km/h) at 27,000 ft (8 230 m); econ cruise, 368 mph (593 km/h) at 41,000 ft (12 500 m); max initial climb, 3,650 ft/min (18,54 m/sec); service ceiling, 44,000 ft (13 410 m); range with IFR reserves (max payload), 1,013 mls (1 630 km), (max fuel), 2,485 mls (4 000 km).

Weights: Operational empty, 6,400 lb (2 903 kg); max take-off, 9,800 lb (4 445 kg).

Accommodation: Pilot and co-pilot/passenger on flight deck and seating for five to nine passengers in main cabin.

Status: First of four flying prototypes scheduled to fly (in Italy) in March 1986, with second (in USA) following in April-May.

Notes: The GP-180 is being developed jointly by Gates Learjet of the USA and Piaggio of Italy, the former being responsible for design and production of the airframe forward of the aft pressure bulkhead, and the latter for the aft fuselage, wing, engine nacelles and tail. Each manufacturer is to establish a final asembly line, with customer deliveries commencing in the last quarter of 1987. The GP-180 is of "three lifting surfaces" concept, a foreplane balancing the aft-located mainplane, a tailplane being retained for pitch control.

GATES-PIAGGIO GP-180

Dimensions: Span, 44 ft 9 in (13,64 m); length, 46 ft 5¾ in (3,91 m); wing area, 169·64 sq ft (15,76 m²).

GENERAL DYNAMICS F-16 FIGHTING FALCON

Country of Origin: USA.

Type: (F-16A) Single-seat multi-role fighter and (F-16B) two-seat operational trainer.

Power Plant: One 14,800 lb st (6713 kgp) dry and 23,830 lb st (10 809 kgp) reheat Pratt & Whitney F100-PW-200 turbofan.

Performance: Max speed (short endurance dash), 1,333 mph (2145 km/h) or Mach = 2·02, (sustained), 1,247 mph (2007 km/h) or Mach = 1·89 at 40,000 ft (12190 m); max cruise, 614 mph (988 km/h) or Mach = 0·93; tactical radius (HI-LO-HI interdiction on internal fuel), 360 mls (580 km) with six 500-lb (227-kg) bombs; range (similar ordnance load and internal fuel), 1,200 mls (1 930 km).

Weights: Operational empty, 14,567 lb (6 613 kg); max take-off, 35,400 lb (16 057 kg).

Armament: One 20-mm M61A-1 multi-barrel rotary cannon and from two to six AIM-9L/M AAMs, or (air support) up to 12,000 lb (5 443 kg) of ordnance between nine stations.

Status: First of two (YF-16) prototypes flown 20 January 1974. First production F-16 flown 7 August 1978, with 1,300 delivered by 1985 by parent company (10 monthly) and European consortium (five monthly), the latter having final assembly lines in Belgium and Netherlands. USAF procurement calls for 2,165 F-16s. European programme embraces 160 for Belgium, 58 for Denmark, 213 for Netherlands and 96 for Norway. Export orders comprise Israel (150), Egypt (80), Greece (40), Pakistan (40), South Korea (36) and Venezuela (24).

Notes: Single-seat F-16C and two-seat F-16D with upgraded systems delivered from July 1984. Commencing 1986, the F-16C/D will have a common engine bay for either the F100 or General Electric F110-GE-100.

GENERAL DYNAMICS F-16 FIGHTING FALCON

Dimensions: Span (excluding missiles), 31 ft 0 in (9,45 m); length, 47 ft 7¾ in (14,52 m); height, 16 ft 5¼ in (5,01 m); wing area, 300 sq ft (27,87 m²).

GRUMMAN E-2C HAWKEYE

Country of Origin: USA.

Type: Airborne early warning, surface surveillance and strike control aircraft.

Power Plant: Two 4,910 ehp Allison T56-A-425 turboprops.

Performance: Max speed, 348 mph (560 km/h) at 10,000 ft (3 050 m); max range cruise, 309 mph (498 km/h); initial climb, 2,515 ft/min (12,8 m/sec); service ceiling, 30,800 ft (9 390 m); mission endurance (at 230 mls/370 km from base), 4·0 hrs; max endurance, 6·1 hrs; ferry range, 1,604 mls (2 580 km).

Weights: Empty, 38,009 lb (17 240 kg); max take-off, 51,900 lb (23 540 kg).

Accommodation: Crew of five comprising flight crew of two and Airborne Tactical Data System team of three, each occupying an independent operating station.

Status: First of two E-2C prototypes flown on 20 January 1971, with first production aircraft flying on 23 September 1972. Some 90 of 103 ordered by US Navy delivered by beginning of 1985, when planned production was scheduled to continue at a rate of six annually into the early 'nineties. Four delivered to Israel, and first four of eight ordered by Japan delivered in 1983. First two of four E-2Cs for Egypt expected to be delivered during 1985.

Notes: The E-2C is the current production version of the Hawkeye, having followed 59 E-2As (all subsequently updated to E-2B standards), and is able to operate independently, in co-operation with other aircraft, or in concert with a ground environment. Two have been delivered to the US Navy as TE-2Cs for use as conversion trainers by the Service's two Hawkeye readiness squadrons which support 12 four-aircraft Hawkeye squadrons attached to the carrier air wings. The E-2X is a simplified export version of the Hawkeye.

GRUMMAN E-2C HAWKEYE

Dimensions: Span, 80 ft 7 in (24,56 m); length, 57 ft 7 in (17,55 m); height, 18 ft 4 in (5,69 m); wing area, 700 sq ft (65,03 m²).

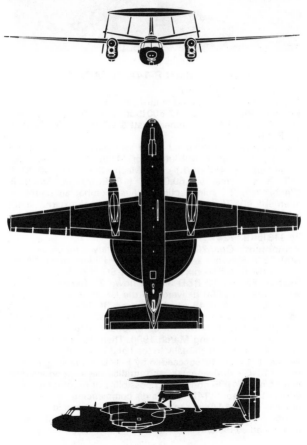

GRUMMAN F-14A TOMCAT

Country of Origin: USA.

Type: Two-seat shipboard multi-role fighter.

Power Plant: Two 12,500 lb st (5 670 kgp) dry and 20,900 lb st (9 840 kgp) reheat Pratt & Whitney TF30-P-412A or -P-414A turbofans.

Performance: Max speed (with four semi-recessed AIM-7 AAMs), 912 mph (1 468 km/h) or Mach=1·2 at sea level, 1,544 mph (2 485 km/h) or Mach=2·34 at 40,000 ft (12 190 m); time to 60,000 ft (18 290 m) at 55,000 lb (24,948 kg), 2·1 min; tactical radius (combat air patrol on internal fuel), 765 mls (1 232 km); range (max external fuel), 2,000 mls (3 220 km).

Weights: Empty, 40,104 lb (18 191 kg); max take-off, 74,348 lb (33 724 kg).

Armament: One 20-mm M61A-1 rotary cannon and six AIM-7E/F Sparrow and four AIM-9G/H Sidewinder AAMs, or six AIM-54A Phoenix and two AIM-9G/H AAMs.

Status: First of 12 R&D aircraft flown 21 December 1970, with more than 500 delivered to the US Navy by beginning of 1985, including 49 as photo-recce RF-14As. Production continuing at rate of 24 annually until 1989, in which year 12 F-14As and 12 F-14Ds will be produced, with deliveries of the latter commencing March 1990. Thereafter production of 30 F-14Ds planned annually to total of 300 aircraft.

Notes: F-14A to be succeeded by F-14D with General Electric F110-GE-400 engines, and studies being conducted at beginning of 1985 concerning possibility or retrofitting about 400 F-14As to F-14D standards commencing in the early nineties. All F-14As are to be cycled through a mid-'eighties avionic update programme, with a new avionics suite being introduced by the end of the decade.

GRUMMAN F-14A TOMCAT

Dimensions: Span (20 deg sweep), 64 ft 1½ in (19,55 m); (68 deg sweep), 37 ft 7 in (11,45 m); length, 61 ft 11⅞ in (18,90 m); height, 16 ft 0 in (4,88 m); wing area, 565 sq ft (52,50 m²).

GRUMMAN X-29A

Country of Origin: USA.

Type: Single seat advanced technology demonstration aircraft.

Power Plant: One 10,600 lb st (4810 kgp) dry and 15,800 lb st (7167 kgp) reheat General Electric F404-GE-400 turbofan.

Performance: Estimated max speed, 1,056 mph (1 700 km/h) or Mach = 1·6 above 36,000 ft (10 975 m).

Weights: (Estimated) Empty, 13,326 lb (6 045 kg); max take-off, 17,303 lb (7 848 kg).

Status: First of two X-29As made its initial flight test on 14 December 1984, commencing a four-month concept evaluation flight programme in April 1985. This is to be followed by an 18-month programme to establish the full flight envelope. The second X-29A is being held in storage unflown as a standby aircraft, and, if necessary, can be readied for flight test within three months.

Notes: The X-29 (Grumman Model 712) is the world's first supersonic aircraft featuring a forward swept wing, and has been developed under a programme primarily funded by the DARPA (Defense Advanced Research Projects Agency) to demonstrate the benefits of forward wing sweep. The X-29A features a digital fly-by-wire system and a thin super-critical wing largely of graphite composite construction, a variable-camber wing trailing edge being mated with all-moving foreplanes (or canard surfaces). Up to 57 per cent of the X-29A consists of off-the-shelf components, these including the front fuselage of the Northrop F-5A, and a flight control system and undercarriage from the General Dynamics F-16A. Forward wing sweep is claimed to offer higher manoeuvrability, improved low-speed handling and lower stalling speeds than the conventional sweptback wing.

GRUMMAN A-29A

Dimensions: Span, 27 ft 2½ in (8,29 m); length (excluding nose probe), 48 ft 1 in (14,66 m); height, 14 ft 3½ in (4,36 m); wing area, 188·84 sq ft (17,54 m²).

GULFSTREAM AEROSPACE GULFSTREAM SRA-1

Country of Origin: USA.

Type: Electronic surveillance, maritime patrol, anti-submarine, transport or medevac aircraft.

Power Plant: Two 11,400 lb st (5 171 kgp) Rolls-Royce RB. 163-25 Spey Mk 511-8 turbofans.

Performance: Max cruise speed, 577 mph (928 km/h); long-range cruise, 509 mph (819 km/h); max operating altitude, 45,000 ft (13 715 m); initial climb, 3,800 ft/min (19,3 m/sec); range with 1,600 lb (726-kg) payload and crew of three at Mach=0·77, 4,030 mls (6 486 km) with IFR reserves, 4,537 mls (7 300 km) with VFR reserves.

Weights: Empty, 32,703 lb (14 831 kg); mission loaded (electronic surveillance), 69 981 lb (31 743 kg), (maritime patrol), 67,924 lb (30 810 kg); max take-off, 69,700 lb (31 600 kg).

Accommodation: Flight crew of two, main cabin arrangements varying according to mission. As a personnel transport up to 18 passengers may be carried, or 15 stretcher patients and medical staff in the aeromedical role.

Status: The prototype Gulfstream SRA-1 was flown on 14 August 1984.

Notes: A special mission version of the Gulfstream III corporate transport (see 1984 edition), three of which have been purchased by the USAF (which plans to purchase eight more) under the designation C-20A, the Gulfstream SRA-1 can be supplied with fully integrated systems for a variety of missions. It features six wing stations for external stores, each capable of carrying up to 2,000 lb (907 kg), provision for a side-looking airborne radar pod beneath the fuselage (as illustrated) and an upward-hinging cargo door in the starboard side of the fuselage.

GULFSTREAM AEROSPACE GULFSTREAM SRA-1

Dimensions: Span, 77 ft 10 in (23,70 m); length, 83 ft 1 in (25,30 m); height, 24 ft 4½ in (7,40 m); wing area, 934·6 sq ft (86,80 m²).

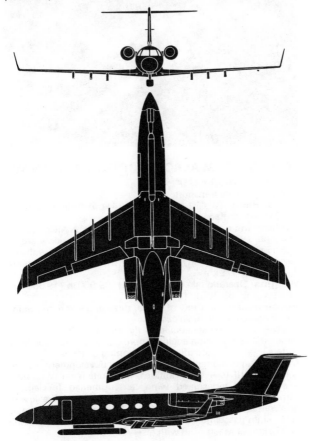

GULFSTREAM AEROSPACE GULFSTREAM IV

Country of Origin: USA.
Type: Corporate transport.
Power Plant: Two 12,420 lb st (5 634 kgp) Rolls-Royce Tay Mk 610-8 turbofans.
Performance: (Manufacturer's estimates) Max speed, 564 mph (908 km/h) at 35,000 ft (10 670 m); econ cruise, 528 mph (850 km/h) at 45,000 ft (13 715 m); range with IFR reserves (max payload), 4,085 mls (6 575 km), (max fuel), 4,954 mls (7 972 km).
Weights: Operational empty (typical), 39,900 lb (18 098 kg); max take-off, 69,700 lb (31 615 kg).
Accommodation: Crew of two or three and standard seating for 19 passengers in main cabin.
Status: Prototype scheduled to fly summer 1985, with customer deliveries commencing approximately one year later. Orders totalled 74 aircraft at the beginning of 1985.
Notes: Fundamentally a progressive development of the Gulfstream III (see 1984 edition), the Gulfstream IV features a structurally redesigned wing, a lengthened fuselage, a carbon-fibre rudder and Tay engines in place of the lower-powered Speys. The range of the Gulfstream IV with two crew, eight passengers and baggage is a guaranteed 4,954 mls (7 972 km) at Mach = 0·8 with reserves.

GULFSTREAM AEROSPACE GULFSTREAM IV

Dimensions: Span, 77 ft 10 in (23,72 m); length, 85 ft 1 in (25,93 m); height, 24 ft 4 in (7,42 m); wing area, 950·39 sq ft (88,29 m²).

GULFSTREAM AEROSPACE PEREGRINE

Country of Origin: USA.

Type: Light corporate transport.

Power Plant: One 3,500 lb st (1 588 kgp) Garrett TFE 731-2 turbofan.

Performance: (Manufacturer's estimates) max cruise speed, 464 mph (747 km/h); normal cruise, 436 mph (702 km/h); at 33,000 ft (10 060 m); initial climb, 3,421 ft/min (17,38 m/sec); service ceiling, 43,270 ft (13 190 m); range (with 45 min reserves), 1,712 mls (2 755 km).

Weights: Empty (with reserve fuel), 5,750 lb (2 608 kg); max take-off, 9,400 lb (4 264 kg).

Accommodation: Pilot and co-pilot/passenger on flight deck and standard main cabin layout for four passengers in club arrangement.

Status: Prototype (illustrated above) flown on 14 January 1983, with production decision taken on 9 February 1984. Production prototype (illustrated on opposite page) scheduled to enter flight test December 1985, with certification and initial customer deliveries planned for second quarter of 1987.

Notes: Unique in being a single-turbofan business executive aircraft and to be certified for single pilot operation, the Peregrine has undergone a power plant change and considerable design revision since initiation of flight test. The original Pratt & Whitney (Canada) JT15D-1 turbofan is being replaced in the production model by the more powerful Garrett TFE 731-2, and changes are being made to the fuselage profile, engine air intake and wing span. Intended primarily for the business manager that flies his own aircraft, the Peregrine offers simple engine handling and no asymmetric complications, its potential market to the end of the decade being forecast as 500-600 units.

GULFSTREAM AEROSPACE PEREGRINE

Dimensions: Span, 45 ft 2 in (13,77 m); length, 41 ft 2 in (12,55 m); height, 15 ft 0 in (4,57 m).

HAL HJT-16 KIRAN II

Country of Origin: India.

Type: Side-by-side two-seat basic trainer and light attack aircraft.

Power Plant: One 3,400 lb st (1 542 kgp) HAL-built Rolls-Royce Orpheus 701-01 turbojet.

Performance: Max speed, 437 mph (704 km/h) at sea level; max cruise, 386 mph (621 km/h) at 15,000 ft (4 575 m); max initial climb, 5 250 ft/min (26,67 m/sec); service ceiling, 39,375 ft (12 000 m); max range (internal fuel), 382 mls (615 km) at 19,680 ft (6 000 m).

Weights: Empty equipped, 6,603 lb (2 995 kg); loaded (clean), 9,347 lb (4 240 kg; max take-off, 10,344 lb (4 692 kg).

Armament: Two 7,62-mm machine guns and provision for up to 2,205 lb (1 000 kg) of ordnance on four wing hardpoints.

Sstatus: First Kiran II prototype flown on 30 July 1976. Series production initiated 1983 agaihnst orders for 60 aircraft from Indian Air Force plus six for Indian Navy. Eighteen delivered by the beginning of 1985.

Notes: The Kiran II is intended primarily for armament training and counter-insurgency tasks, and differs from the Kiran I in having a more powerful engine (an Orpheus supplanting the Viper of the Kirans I and IA), improved weapons carrying capability, updated avionics and an improved hydraulics system. The original Kiran first flew on 4 September 1964.

HAL HJT-16 KIRAN II

Dimensions: Span, 35 ft 1¼ in (10,70 m); length, 33 ft 7½ in (10,60 m); height, 11 ft 11 in (3,64 m); wing area, 204·5 sq ft (19,00 m²).

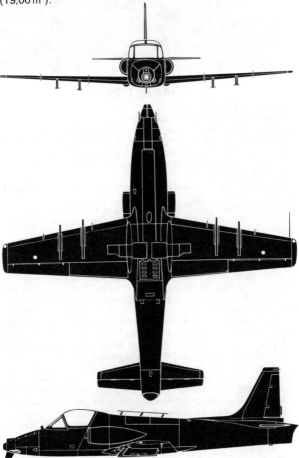

HAL HTT-34

Country of Origin: India.

Type: Side-by-side two-seat trainer.

Power Plant: One 420 shp Allison 250-B17D turboprop.

Performance: Max speed, 162 mph (261 km/h) at 9,840 ft (3 000 m); max initial climb, 2,000 ft/min (10,16 m/sec); service ceiling, 26,000 ft (7 925 m); range, 280 mls (450 km) at 10,000 ft (3 050 m).

Weights: Empty, 1,884 lb (855 kg); max take-off, 2,689 lb (1 220 kg).

Status: Prototype HTT-34 (converted from third prototype HPT-32) flown on 17 June 1984, and development continuing at beginning of 1985.

Notes: The HTT-34 is a derivative of the piston-engined HPT-32 (see 1983 edition) currently in production for the Indian Air Force and is fundamentally similar to the earlier aircraft apart from extended engine bearers to restore the CG position to that of the HPT-32. The HTT-34 is being developed as a company-funded programme and if ordered by the Indian Air Force is expected to have a fully-retractable undercarriage which is being offered as an option, and updated instrumentation and avionics. Fifty of the earlier HPT-32 are currently on order (the first having been handed over on 31 March 1984), and current planning calls for a follow-on of a further 90 aircraft, but it is considered likely that the follow-on batch will be delivered as HTT-34s. Smaller and lighter than most contemporary turboprop-powered trainers (the exception being the Siai Marchetti SF 260TP—see 1983 edition), the HTT-34 is unique among such aircraft in having a fixed undercarriage. It is fully aerobatic at maximum take-off weight.

HAL HTT-34

Dimensions: Span, 31 ft 2 in (9,50 m); length, 26 ft 5¾ in (8,07 m); height, 9 ft 5½ in (2,88 m); wing aarea, 161·5 sq ft (15,00 m²).

HUNTING FIRECRACKER

Country of Origin: United Kingdom.
Type: Tandem two-seat basic/advanced trainer.
Power Plant: One 550 shp (flat-rated) Pratt & Whitney (Canada) PT6A-25A turboprop.
Performance: Max speed, 228 mph (367 km/h) at 15,000 ft (4 575 m); econ cruise, 207 mph (333 km/h) at 20,000 ft (6 100 m); max initial climb, 2,060 ft/min (10,46 m/sec); service ceiling, 27,100 ft (8 260 m); range (standard fuel and no reserves), 720 mls (1 158 km), (with two 32 Imp gal/145 l non-jettisonable external auxiliary tanks), 1,266 mls, (2 038 km).
Weights: Empty equipped, 2,350 lb (1 066 kg) max take-off, 3,600 lb (1 633 kg).
Status: Known originally as the NDN-1T Turbo Firecracker, the first prototype was flown on 1 September 1983. This and second aircraft acquired by Specialist Flying Training. Development taken over by Hunting Firecracker Aircraft from 1 September 1984.
Notes: The Firecracker was a contender for the RAF order to meet the requirements of AST (Air Staff Target) 412. Whereas the data above apply to the aircraft in its certificated civil form, the Firecracker as submitted for AST 412 featured a 750 shp PT6A-25D engine, a Stencel Ranger zero-zero rocket escape system, a revised wing and increased internal fuel capacity. Empty equipped weight was raised to 2,667 lb (1 210 kg) and max take-off weight to 4,040 lb (1 832 kg), these increases being accompanied by gains in take-off, climb and level speed performance. The Firecracker as illustrated features a unique low aspect ratio wing intended to reproduce the roll yaw characteristics and low-speed sink rates of pure-jet swept- and delta-wing combat aircraft.

HUNTING FIRECRACKER

Dimensions: Span, 26 ft 0 in (7,92 m); length, 27 ft 4 in (8,33 m); height, 10 ft 8 in (3,25 m); wing area, 128 sq ft (11,89 m²).

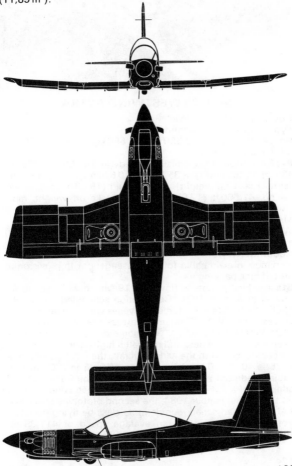

IAI 1125 WESTWIND ASTRA

Country of Origin: Israel.
Type: Light corporate transport.
Power Plant: Two 3,650 lb st (1 656 kgp) Garrett TFE731-3B-100G turbofans.
Performance: Max cruising speed (at 16,000 lb/7 258 kg), 535 mph (862 km/h) at 35,000 ft (10 670 m); max initial climb (at max take-off weight), 3,560 ft/min (18,08 m/sec); service ceiling, 41,500 ft (12 650 m) at max take-off weight; range (two crew and five passengers), 2,935 mls (4 723 km) at Mach = 0·8, 3,580 mls (5 760 km) at long-range cruise.
Weights: Basic operating (typical), 12,670 lb (5 747 kg); max take-off, 23,500 lb (10 660 kg).
Accommodation: Flight crew of two and standard accommodation in main cabin for six passengers, with provision for max of nine passengers.
Status: First prototype flown on 19 March with second following in August 1984. Certification scheduled for October 1985, at which time customer deliveries will commence.
Notes: The IAI 1125 retains the fuselage of the earlier IAI 1124 Westwind II, which, with some design refinement, has been mated with a new and relocated high-speed swept wing. By comparison with the earlier aircraft, the fuselage of the IAI 1125 is 40 in (102 cm) longer and offers 8 in (20 cm) more cabin headroom as a result of reshaping the frames and the adoption of a low- rather than mid-positioned wing. Between 24 and 29 September 1984, the second prototype established FAI-recognised speed records in its class by flying from New York to Los Angeles at an average speed of 411·39 mph (662 km/h) and back at 554·34 mph (892 km/h).

IAI 1125 WESTWIND ASTRA

Dimension: Span, 52 ft 8 in (16.05 m); length, 55 ft 7 in (16,94 m); height, 18 ft 2 in (5,53 m); wing area, 316·6 sq ft (29,41 m²).

IAv CRAIOVA IAR-99 SOIM

Country of Origin: Romania.

Type: Tandem two-seat advanced trainer and light attack aircraft.

Power Plant: One 4,000 lb st (1 814 kgp) Tubomecanica-built Rolls-Royce Viper Mk 632-41 turbojet.

Performance: Max speed (at 12,072 lb/5 476 kg), 537 mph (865 km/h) at sea level or Mach=0·783, 502 mph (808 km/h) at 30,000 ft (9 145 m); max initial climb, 7,185 ft/min (36,5 m/sec); service ceiling, 45,600 ft (13 900 m).

Weights: Empty equipped, 6,878 lb (3 120 kg); max take-off, 12,072 lb (5 476 kg).

Armament: Four wing hardpoints of 772 lb (350 kg) capacity inboard and 551 lb (250 kg) capacity outboard for rocket packs, gun pods and light bombs, and provision beneath fuselage for one 23-mm GSh-23L twin-barrel cannon pod.

Status: Prototype testing initiated late 1982/early 1983. No details available of production status at beginning of 1985, but reported that the Romanian Air Force has a requirement for 100–150 aircraft in this category.

Notes: The Soim (Hawk) has been designed and built by the Intreprinderea de Avioane (IAv) at Craiova to meet a requirement for an advanced pilot training aircraft with secondary ground attack capabilities drawn up by the Romanian Air Force in the late 'seventies. The Soim is intended to carry pilots from such piston-engined trainers as the IAR-823 to two-seat conversion training versions of combat aircraft types, such as the MiG-21U and MiG-23U, and the two-seat variant of the IAR-93A attack aircraft.

IAv CRAIOVA IAR-99 SOIM

Dimensions: Span, 32 ft 3¼ in (9,85 m); length, 35 ft 8¼ in (10,88 m); height, 12 ft 9 in (3,89 m); wing area, 201·4 sq ft (18,71 m²).

ILYUSHIN (MAINSTAY)

Country of Origin: USSR.

Type: Airborne warning and control system aircraft.

Power Plant: Four 26,455 lb st (12 000 kgp) Soloviev D-30KP turbofans.

Performance: (Estimated) Max cruise speed, 475 mph (764 km/h) at 29,500-42,650 ft (9 000-13 000 m); loiter speed, 390-410 mph (630-660 km/h) at 29,500 ft (9 000 m); time on station (unrefuelled) at 930 mls (1 500 km) from base, 6-7 hrs.

Weights: (Estimated) Max take-off, 380,000 lb (172 370 kg).

Accommodation: Probable flight crew of four with tactical and air direction teams totalling 9-10 personnel.

Status: Mainstay has been derived from the Il-76 freighter and is known to have been under test since 1979-80. Mainstay will attain initial operational status during 1985, five-six having been in service by the beginning of the year, and some 30 will be in service by 1986-7.

Notes: A derivative of the Il-76 (see 1983 edition), Mainstay is believed to differ from the freighter primarily in having an over-fuselage "saucer" rotating radome with AWACS avionics in the main cabin, some nominal lengthening of the forward fuselage and provision for flight refuelling. Mainstay is intended to replace the Tu-126 Moss which possessed only limited capability over land, and will be used to vector interceptors with lookdown/shootdown capability towards low-level penetrating aircraft. The Foxhound (see pages 156-7) is apparently optimised for operation with Mainstay. Production of the Il-76 transport for both military and commercial use was continuing at the beginning of 1985 at approximately 30-35 annually, with some 220-250 delivered.

ILYUSHIN (MAINSTAY)

Dimensions: (Estimated) Span, 165 ft 8⅓ in (50,50 m); length, 155 ft 9 in (47,50 m); height, 48 ft 5 in (14,76 m); wing area, 3,299·2 sq ft (300,00 m²).

ILYUSHIN IL-86 (CAMBER)

Country of Origin: USSR.

Type: Medium-haul commercial airliner.

Power Plant: Four 28,660 lb st (13 000 kgp) Kuznetsov NK-86 turbofans.

Performance: Max cruising speed, 590 mph (950 km/h) at 29,530 ft (9 000 m); econ cruise, 559 mph (900 km/h) at 36,090 ft (11 000 m); range (with max payload—350 passengers), 2,485 mls (4 000 km), (with 250 passengers), 3,107 mls (5 000 km).

Weights: Max take-off, 454,150 lb (206 000 kg).

Accommodation: Basic flight crew of three-four and up to 350 passengers nine-abreast with two aisles and divided between three cabins seating 111, 141 and 98 passengers.

Status: First prototype flown on 22 December 1976, and production prototype flown on 24 October 1977. Deliveries to Aeroflot commenced 1980, and some 40 are believed to have been delivered by the beginning of 1985. The Polish WSK-Mielec concern is responsible for manufacture of the entire wing, stabiliser and engine pylons. Four Il-86s were originally to have been delivered to Polish Airlines LOT.

Notes: The Il-86 operated its first scheduled service (Moscow–Tashkent) on 26 December 1980, and first international service (Moscow–Prague) on 12 October 1981, but there has been an unexplained slippage in Aeroflot's programmed introduction of the Il-86 on many routes and it is believed that performance has fallen short of expectations. It is expected that production will be restricted in favour of the longer-range derivative type, the Il-96, which it is anticipated will be powered by the new D-18T turbofan in the 50,700 lb st (23 000 kgp) category. Sub-assemblies for the Il-96 are to be manufactured by the WSK-Mielec in Poland under a collaborative agreement, and this intended successor to the Il-86 is scheduled to enter service in the late 'eighties.

ILYUSHIN IL-86 (CAMBER)

Dimensions: Span, 157 ft 8⅛ in (48,06 m); length, 195 ft 4 in (59,54 m); height, 51 ft 10½ in (15,81 m); wing area, 3,550 sq ft (329,80 m²).

KAWASAKI XT-4

Country of Origin: Japan.

Type: Tandem two-seat basic trainer.

Power Plant: Two 3,660 lb st (1 660 kgp) Ishikawajima-Harima XF3-30 turbofans.

Performance: (Manufacturer's estimates) Max speed (with 50% fuel), 622 mph (1 000 km/h) at 25,000 ft (7 620 m) or Mach=0·9, 576 mph (927 km/h) at sea level; cruising speed (max internal fuel), 506 mph (815 km/h) at 30,000 ft (9 145 m) or Mach=0·75; range, 863 mls (1 390 km), with two 100 Imp gal (455 l) drop tanks, 1,036 mls (1 668 km).

Weights: Empty, 8,157 lb (3 700 kg); loaded clean, 12,125 lb (5 500 kg); max take-off, 16,535 lb (7 500 kg).

Status: The first of four prototypes is scheduled to enter flight test in July 1985, the remaining prototypes following in December 1985, and January and February 1986. The first 49 of proposed procurement of about 200 aircraft for the Japanese Air Self-Defence Force are included in the 1983–87 defence plan, and production is expected to commence in Fiscal 1986 and continue at a rate of 40 annually for five years.

Notes: The XT-4 is being developed by Kawasaki as prime contractor, Mitsubishi being responsible for the centre and rear fuselage, the engine air intakes and the vertical tail, and Fuji being responsible for the wings and nose. There will be provision for five external pylons for drop tanks, target-towing equipment, chaff dispensers, or for gun pods, practice bombs or IR missiles for armament training. The XT-4 is intended primarily as a successor to the Fuji T-1, but, in addition to pilot training, will fulfil various other duties, including liaison.

KAWASAKI XT-4

Dimensions: (Approximate) Span, 32 ft 9¾ in (10,00 m); length, 42 ft 8 in (13,00 m); height, 16 ft 5 in (5,00 m); wing area, 232·5 sq ft (21,60 m²).

LOCKHEED L-100-30 HERCULES

Country of Origin: USA.
Type: Medium/long-range military and commercial freight transport.
Power Plant: Four 4,508 ehp Allison T56-A-15 turboprops.
Performance: Max cruise speed, 386 mph (620 km/h) at 20,000 ft (6 095 m); long-range cruise, 345 mph (556 km/h); range (max. payload), 2,300 mls (3 700 km); ferry range (with 2,265 Imp gal/10 296 l of external fuel), 5,354 mls (8 617 km).
Weights: Operational empty, 79,516 lb (36 068 kg); max take-off, 155,000 lb (70 310 kg).
Accommodation: Normal flight crew of four and provision for 97 casualty litters plus medical attendants, 128 combat troops or 92 paratroops. For pure freight role up to seven cargo pallets may be loaded.
Status: A total of 1,735 Hercules (all versions) against orders for 1,776 had been delivered by the beginning of 1985 when production was continuing at three monthly.
Notes: The L-100-30 and its military equivalent, the C-130H-30, are stretched versions of the basic Hercules, the C-130H. The original civil model, the L-100-20 featured a 100-in (2,54-m) fuselage stretch over the basic military model, and the L-100-30, intended for both military and civil application, embodies a further 80-in (2,03-m) stretch. Military operators of the C-130H-30 version are Algeria, Indonesia, Ecuador, Cameroun and Nigeria, and 30 of the RAF's Hercules C Mk 1s (equivalent of the C-130H) are being modified to C-130H-30 standards as Hercules C Mk 3s, most having been returned to service by the beginning 1985. Some 40 variants of the Hercules have so far been produced and this type now serves (in military and civil roles) with 57 countries.

LOCKHEED L-100-30 HERCULES

Dimensions: Span, 132 ft 7 in (40,41 m); length, 112 ft 9 in (34,37 m); height, 38 ft 3 in (11,66 m); wing area, 1,745 sq ft (162,12 m²).

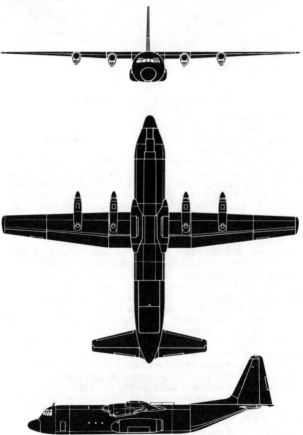

LOCKHEED C-5B GALAXY

Country of Origin: USA.

Type: Heavy strategic transport.

Power Plant: Four 41,100 lb st (18 643 kgp) General Electric TF39-GE-1C turbofans.

Performance: Max speed, 571 mph (919 km/h) at 25,000 ft (7 620 m); max cruise, 552–564 mph (888–908 km/h) at 25,000 ft (7 620 m); econ cruise, 518 mph (833 km/h); max initial climb, 1,725 ft/min (8,75 m/sec); range (with max payload), 2,728 mls (4 390 km), (max fuel and reserves), 6,850 mls (11 024 km).

Weights: Operational empty, 374,000 lb (169 643 kg); max take-off, 769,000 lb (348 820 kg).

Accommodation: Flight crew of five plus 15 seats on flight deck, 75 seats in aft troop compartment and up to 270 troops on pallet-mounted seats in cargo compartment. Up to 36 standard 463L cargo pallets, or various vehicles.

Status: First flight of C-5B scheduled for 12 September and first delivery to USAF planned late November 1985 against requirement for 50 aircraft. Production is to peak in January 1988 at two per month with the 23rd aircraft.

Notes: Production of 81 examples of the C-5A (illustrated above) was completed in May 1973, manufacture of the Galaxy being reinstated in 1982 with the C-5B. Although external aerodynamic configuration and internal arrangements remain unchanged between the C-5A and C-5B, the latter differs in respect of some items of equipment and incorporates from the outset various significant improvements already made on or proposed for the rewinged C-5As, all 77 of which will have passed through the rewinging programme by July 1987.

LOCKHEED C-5B GALAXY

Dimensions: Span, 222 ft 8½ in (67,88 m); length, 247 ft 10 in (75,53 m); height, 65 ft 1½ in (19,34 m); wing area, 6,200 sq ft (575,98 m²).

LOCKHEED P-3 (AEW&C) ORION

Country of Origin: USA.

Type: Airborne warning and control system aircraft.

Power Plant: Four 4,910 ehp Allison T56-A-14 or (proposed) T56-A-427 turboprops.

Performance: Max cruising speed, 410 mph (660 km/h) at 15,000 ft (4 570 m); econ cruise, 373 mph (600 km/h) at 25,000 ft (7 620 m); average loiter speed, 240 mph (386 km/h) at 25,000 ft (7 620 m); time on station (unrefuelled), 8·5 hrs at 920 mls (1 480 km) from base; max range, 4,836 mls (7 783 km); max endurance, 14 hrs.

Weights: Empty, 68,554 lb (31 096 kg); max take-off, 134,770 lb (61 132 kg).

Status: Prototype (converting from P-3B) first flown on 13 June 1984. Development being pursued as a private venture at beginning of 1985.

Notes: The P-3 (AEW&C) version of the Orion maritime patrol and ASW aircraft is intended to fulfil the requirements of an emerging export market for airborne warning and control system aircraft. The prototype, an ex-RAAF P-3B, is being fitted with a General Electric AN/APS-138 radar (similar to that of the Grumman E-2C Hawkeye) during the course of 1985 following the completion of aerodynamic, performance and loading trials. The revolving radome mounted above the rear fuselage has a diameter of 24 ft (7,32 m). Approximately 590 Orions of various models had been delivered by the beginning of 1985.

LOCKHEED P-3 (AEW&C) ORION

Dimensions: Span, 99 ft 8 in (30,37 m); length, 107 ft 7½ in (32,80 m); height, 33 ft 8½ in (10,27 m); wing area, 1,300 sq ft (120,77 m²).

McDONNELL DOUGLAS AV-8B HARRIER II

Country of Origin: USA (and UK).

Type: Single-seat V/STOL ground attack aircraft.

Power Plant: One 21,550 lb st (9 775 kgp) Rolls-Royce F402-RR-406 Pegasus 11-21 E (Mk 105) turbofan.

Performance: Max speed (clean aircraft) 668 mph (1 075 km/h) or Mach=0·88 at sea level, 614 mph (988 km/h) or Mach=0·93 at 36,000 ft (10 970 m); tactical radius (HI-LO-HI interdiction with seven 1,000-lb/453,6-kg bombs and 25-mm cannon), 692 mls (1 114 km); ferry range (with four 250 Imp/gal/1 136 l drop tanks), 2,876 mls (4 630 km).

Weights: Operational empty, 12,750 lb (5 783 kg); max take-off (for VTO), 19,185 lb (8 702 kg), (for STO), 29,750 lb (13 495 kg).

Armament: One 25-mm GAU-12/U five-barrel rotary cannon and up to 9,200 lb (4 173 kg) of ordnance on one fuselage centreline and six wing stations.

Status: First of four FSD (Full Scale Development) aircraft flown on 5 November 1981, with first of pilot batch of 12 aircraft for the US Marine Corps flown on 29 August 1983. The USMC has a requirement for 336 aircraft, and the RAF has an initial requirement for a further 62 (as Harrier GR Mk 5s), the first of which is scheduled to fly spring 1985, with deliveries scheduled for 1986. Twelve AV-8Bs are to be delivered to Spain from late 1986.

Notes: The AV-8B is a progressive development of the British Aerospace Harrier (see 1982 edition) currently serving with the RAF in GR Mk 3 and T Mk 4 forms, with USMC as the AV-8C and TAV-8A, and with the Spanish Navy as the Matador. The AV-8B Harrier II differs primarily in having a larger supercritical wing of composite construction, improved lift devices, extended rear fuselage and a raised cockpit. It has twice the payload or action radius of the Harrier GR Mk 3.

McDONNELL DOUGLAS AV-8B HARRIER II

Dimensions: Span, 30 ft 4 in (9,24 m); length, 46 ft 4 in (14,12 m); height, 11 ft 8 in (3,55 m); wing area, 241 sq ft (22,40 m²).

McDONNELL DOUGLAS F-15C EAGLE

Country of Origin: USA.
Type: Single-seat air superiority fighter.
Power Plant: Two 14,780 lb st (6705 kgp) dry and 23,904 lb st (10855 kgp) reheat Pratt & Whitney F100-PW-100 turbofans.
Performance: Max speed (short-endurance dash), 1,676 mph (2698 km/h) or Mach=2·54, (sustained), 1,518 mph (2443 km/h) or Mach=2·3 at 40,000 ft (12190 m); max endurance (internal fuel), 2·9 hrs, (with conformal pallets), 5·25 hrs; service ceiling, 63,000 ft (19200 m).
Weights: Basic equipped, 28,700 lb (13018 kg); loaded (full internal fuel and four AIM-7 AAMs), 44,500 lb (20185 kg); max take-off, 68,000 lb (30845 kg).
Armament: One 20-mm M-61A1 rotary cannon plus four AIM-7F Sparrow and four AIM-9L Sidewinder AAMs.
Status: First flown 26 February 1979, the F-15C is the second major single-seat production version of the Eagle, having, together with its two-seat equivalent, the F-15D, supplanted the F-15A and F-15B from the 444th aircraft mid 1980. The F-15C and D were the current production models at the beginning of 1985, with more than 870 (all versions) delivered, total USAF Eagle requirement being 1,488 aircraft, including 392 of the dual-role F-15E for delivery from 1988.
Notes: Featuring upgraded avionics and conformal fuel packs, the F-15C is being supplied to Saudi Arabia (47 plus 15 F-15Ds) and 155 are being licence manufactured as F-15Js by Japan (including eight from knocked-down assemblies) which country is also receiving 12 F-15DJ two-seaters. Israel received 40 F-15 Eagles (since modified for conformal tanks) and is to receive a further 11 aircraft.

McDONNELL DOUGLAS F-15C EAGLE

Dimensions: Span, 42 ft 9¾ in (13,05 m); length, 63 ft 9 in (19,43 m); height, 18 ft 5½ in (5,63 m); wing area, 608 sq ft (56,50 m²).

McDONNELL DOUGLAS F/A-18A HORNET

Country of Origin: USA.

Type: Single-seat shipboard and shore-based multi-role fighter and attack aircraft.

Power Plant: Two 10,600 lb st (4 810 kgp) dry and 15,800 lb st (7 167 kgp) reheat General Electric F404-GE-400 turbofans.

Performance: Max speed (AAMs on wingtip and fuselage stations), 1,190 mph (1 915 km/h) or Mach = 1·8 at 40,000 ft (12 150 m); initial climb (half fuel and wingtip AAMs), 60,000 ft/min (304,6 m/sec); tactical radius (combat air patrol on internal fuel), 480 mls (770 km), (with three 262 Imp gal/ 1 192 l external tanks), 735 mls (1 180 km).

Weights: Empty equipped, 28,000 lb (12 700 kg); loaded (air superiority mission with half fuel and four AAMs), 35,800 lb (16 240 kg); max take-off, 56,000 lb (25 400 kg).

Armament: One 20-mm M-61A-1 rotary cannon and (air-air) two AIM-7E/F Sparrow and two AIM-9G/H Sidewinder AAMs, or (attack) up to 17,000 lb (7 711 kg) of ordnance.

Status: First of 11 FSD (full-scale development) Hornets (including two TF-18A two-seaters) flown 18 November 1978. Planning at beginning of 1984 called for 1,366 Hornets for US Navy and US Marine Corps (including 153 TF-18As). First production F/A-18A flown April 1980.

Notes: Land-based versions of the Hornet have been ordered by Australia (57 F/A-18As and 18 TF-18As), Canada (113 CF-18As and 24 CF-18Bs) and Spain (72 EF-18As and TF-18As). Separate F-18 fighter and A-18 attack versions of the Hornet were initially planned by the US Navy. Both roles were subsequently combined in a single basic version, and current planning calls for the inclusion of two Hornet squadrons in the complement of each of the large US Navy carriers.

McDONNELL DOUGLAS F/A-18A HORNET

Dimensions: Span, 37 ft 6 in (11,43 m); length, 56 ft 0 in (17,07 m); height, 15 ft 4 in (4,67 m); wing area, 396 sq ft (36,79 m²).

McDONNELL DOUGLAS KC-10A EXTENDER

Country of Origin: USA.

Type: Flight refuelling tanker and military freighter.

Power Plant: Three 52,500 lb st (23 814 kgp) General Electric CF6-50C2 turbofans.

Performance: Max speed, 620 mph (988 km/h) at 33,000 ft (10 060 m); max cruise, 595 mph (957 km/h) at 31,000 ft (9 450 m); long-range cruise, 540 mph (870 km/h); typical refuelling mission, 2,200 mls (3 540 km) from base with 200,000 lb (90 720 kg) of fuel and return; max range (with 170,000 lb/77 112 kg freight), 4,370 mls (7 033 km).

Weights: Operational empty (tanker), 239,747 lb (108 749 kg), (cargo configuration), 243,973 lb (110 660 kg); max take-off, 590,000 lb (267 624 kg).

Accommodation: Flight crew of five plus provision for six seats for additional crew and four bunks for crew rest. Fourteen further seats may be provided for support personnel in the forward cabin. Alternatively, a larger area can be provided for 55 more support personnel, with necessary facilities, to increase total accommodation (including flight crew) to 80.

Status: First KC-10A was flown on 12 July 1980, with 16 ordered by the USAF by the beginning of 1983. A further 44 have been ordered under five-year contracting process for delivery through 1987. First operational KC-10A squadron was activated on 1 October 1981, and 28 had been delivered to the USAF by the beginning of 1985.

Notes: The KC-10A is a military tanker/freighter derivative of the commercial DC-10 Series 30 (see 1983 edition) with refuelling boom, boom operator's station, hose and drogue, and body fuel cells in the lower cargo compartments.

McDONNELL DOUGLAS KC-10A EXTENDER

Dimensions: Span, 165 ft 4 in (50,42 m); length, 182 ft 0 in (55,47 m); height, 58 ft 1 in (17,70 m); wing area, 3,958 sq ft (367,7 m²).

McDONNELL DOUGLAS MD-80

Country of Origin: USA.
Type: Short/medium-haul commercial airliner.
Power Plant: (MD-81) Two 19,250 lb st (8730 kgp) Pratt & Whitney JT8D-209 turbofans.
Performance: Max cruising speed, 574 mph (924 km/h) at 27,000 ft (8230 m); econ cruise, 522 mph (840 km/h) at 33,000 ft (10060 m); long-range cruise, 505 mph (813 km/h) at 35,000 ft (10670 m); range (with max payload), 1,594 mls (2565 km) at econ cruise, (with max fuel), 3,280 mls (5280 km) at long-range cruise.
Weights: Operational empty, 77,797 lb (35289 kg); max take-off, 140,000 lb (63503 kg).
Accommodation: Flight crew of two and typical mixed-class arrangement for 23 first- and 137 economy-class passengers, or 155 all-economy or 172 commuter-type arrangements with five-abreast seating.
Status: First MD-80 flown (as Super 80) on 18 October 1979, with first customer delivery (to Swissair) on 12 September 1980, and 500 ordered by beginning of 1985 with 195 delivered, production being four monthly.
Notes: The MD-80 is the largest of six members of the DC-9 family, the MD-82 sub-type having 20,850 lb st (9458 kgp) JT8D-217 engines with which it was certificated at a max take-off weight of 149,500 lb (67813 kg) in September 1982, this giving a max payload range of 2,300 mls (3700 km). The MD-83 with a max take-off weight of 160,000 lb (72576 kg) and a max payload range of the order of 2,880 mls (4630 km), was flown on 17 December 1984, with first customer deliveries (to Alaska) commencing 1985. Overall size remains unchanged, but wings and undercarriage have been strengthened to cater for the additional fuel and increased weights. The MD-87, launched at the beginning of 1985, has a 17 ft 5 in (5,30 m) shorter fuselage, JT8D-217B engines and capacity for 130–139 passengers. Deliveries will commence in 1986.

McDONNELL DOUGLAS MD-80

Dimension: Span, 107 ft 10 in (32,85 m); length, 147 ft 10 in (45,08 m); height, 29 ft 4 in (8,93 m); wing area, 1,279 sq ft (118,8 m²).

MIKOYAN MIG-23 (FLOGGER)

Country of Origin: USSR.

Type: Single-seat (Flogger-B, E and G) air superiority and (Flogger-F and H) close air support fighter.

Power Plant: One 17,635 lb st (8000 kgp) dry and 25,350 lb st (11 500 kgp) reheat Tumansky R-29B turbojet.

Performance: (Flogger-G) Max speed (clean aircraft with half fuel), 1,520 mph (2 446 km/h) or Mach = 2·3 above 36,090 ft (11 000 m); combat radius (high-altitude air-air mission with four AAMs), 530 mls (850 km), (with centreline combat tank), 700 mls.

Weights: Normal loaded (clean), 34,170 lb (15 500 kg); max take-off, 44,312 lb (20 100 kg).

Armament: One 23-mm twin-barrel GSh-23L cannon and (B and G) two AA-7 Apex and two AA-8 Aphid, or (E) four AA-2-2 Advanced Atoll AAMs, or (F and H) up to 9,920 lb (4 500 kg) of bombs and missiles.

Status: Aerodynamic prototype of MiG-23 flown winter 1966-67, with service debut (Flogger-B) following 1971. Production rate of 35 (all versions) monthly continuing at beginning of 1985, when some 2,600 were estimated to be in Soviet service.

Notes: The Flogger-G (illustrated) is the latest air-air version of the MiG-23 in Soviet service, this being an improved variant of the Flogger-B (see 1982 edition) with revised vertical tail and other changes. Flogger-E is an export equivalent of Flogger-B, and Flogger-F and H are air-ground versions with redesigned forward fuselage essentially similar to that of the MiG-27 (see pages 152-3).

MIKOYAN MIG-23 (FLOGGER)

Dimensions: (Estimated) Span (17 deg sweep), 46 ft 9in (14,25 m), (72 deg sweep), 27 ft 6 in (8,38 m); length (including probe), 55 ft 1½ in (16,80 m); wing area, 293·4 sq ft (27,26 m²).

MIKOYAN MIG-27 (FLOGGER)

Country of Origin: USSR.

Type: Single-seat tactical strike and close air support fighter.

Power Plant: One 14,330 lb st (6 500 kgp) dry and 17,920 lb st (8 130 kgp) reheat Tumansky R-29-300 turbojet.

Performance: Max speed (clean aircraft with half fuel), 685 mph (1 102 km/h) or Mach=0·95 at 1,000 ft (305 m), 1,056 mph (1 700 km/h) or Mach=1·6 at 36,090 ft (11 000 m); combat radius (HI-LO-HI mission profile on internal fuel with 4,410 lb/2 000 kg ordnance), 310 mls (500 km).

Weights: (Estimated) Normal loaded (clean), 35,000 lb (15 875 kg); max take-off, 45,000 lb (20 410 kg).

Armament: One 23-mm six-barrel rotary cannon and up to 7,716 lb (3 500 kg) of external ordnance on five stations.

Status: Evolved from the MiG-23 (see pages 150-1) as a dedicated air-ground aircraft, the MiG-27 is believed to have first entered service (in Flogger-D) form in 1975-76, with production continuing (in Flogger-J form) as MiG-27M at the beginning of 1985. Licence production is undertaken in India with first completed (from CKD kit) in October 1984.

Notes: Whereas the Flogger-F and H are minimum-change air-ground derivatives of the MiG-23, the MiG-27 has been tailored closely for ground attack. The forward fuselage is similar to that of the Flogger-F and H, apart from augmented side armour, but the rough-field undercarriage has necessitated bulging of the fuselage and a modified turbofan is installed with larger-area fixed intakes and shorter afterburner nozzle. The Flogger-J (illustrated) has a lengthened nose and wing leading-edge extensions.

MIKOYAN MIG-27 (FLOGGER)

Dimensions: (Estimated) Span (17 deg sweep), 46 ft 9 in (14,25 m), (72 deg sweep), 27 ft 6 in (8,38 m); length, 54 ft 0 in (16,46 m); wing area, 293·4 sq ft (27,26 m²).

MIKOYAN MIG-29 (FULCRUM)

Country of Origin: USSR.

Type: Single-seat counterair fighter.

Power Plant: Two 11,243 lb st (5 100 kgp) dry and 18,300 lb st (8 300 kgp) reheat Tumansky R-33D turbofans.

Performance: (Estimated) Max speed, 1,518 mph (2 445 km/h) above 36,100 ft (11 000 m), or Mach = 2·3, 915 mph (1 470 km/h) at sea level, or Mach = 1·2; max initial climb, 50,000 ft/min (254 m/sec); combat radius (four AAMs), 415 mls (670 km), (four 1,100-lb/500-kg bombs), 375 mls (600 km).

Weights: (Estimated) Operational empty, 18,000 lb (8 165 kg); max take-off, 36,000 lb (16 330 kg).

Armament: One 30-mm cannon and six AA-10 AAMs.

Status: First seen in prototype form in 1979, the MiG-29 attained initial operational capability in 1984, exports being scheduled to commence November 1985 when the Indian Air Force anticipates receiving 40 aircraft. A further 150 are scheduled to be licence-built in India (initially from CKD kits) with deliveries commencing 1987–88.

Notes: The MiG-29 features a new long-range track-while-scan radar, a pulse Doppler lookdown/shootdown weapon system, infrared search and tracking, and a digital data link. Its primary armament is expected to eventually consist of AA-10 medium-range AAMs, but those for India will have two R-23R (Apex) and four R-60 (Aphid) air-to-air missiles.

MIKOYAN MIG-29 (FULCRUM)

Dimensions: (Estimated) Span, 34 ft 5 in (10,50 m); length (including probe), 50 ft 10 in (15,50 m); height, 17 ft 2 in (5,25 m); wing area, 380 sq ft (35,30 m²).

MIKOYAN MIG-31 (FOXHOUND)

Country of Origin: USSR.

Type: Tandem two-seat interceptor fighter.

Power Plant: Two 30,865 lb st (14 000 kgp) reheat Tumansky turbojets.

Performance: (Estimated) Max speed, 1,520 mph (2 445 km/h) above 36,100 ft (11 000 m), or Mach = 2·3, 915 mph (1 472 km/h) at sea level; max operational radius (with external fuel), 1,180 mls (1 900 km); ceiling 80,000 ft (24 385 m).

Weights: (Estimated) Empty equipped, 45,000 lb (20 410 kg); normal loaded, 65,200 lb (29 575 kg)

Armament: Up to eight AA-9 radar-guided AAMs.

Status: The MiG-31 has been under development since the mid 'seventies and is believed to have been first deployed in 1982, with several regiments equipped with this type by the beginning of 1985.

Notes: The MiG-31 has been derived from the MiG-25 (see 1984 Edition) and features a redesigned forward fuselage housing a lookdown-shootdown pulse Doppler weapons system and tandem cockpits for the pilot and systems operator. Some indication of the capability of the MiG-31 came in 1978, when a Soviet official announcement indicated that, during tests, presumably a prototype flying at around 6 000 m (19 685 ft) had detected a target flying below 60 m (200 ft) at a range of 20 km (12·5 mls), fired an unarmed missile against it and achieved a theoretical kill. The Tumansky engines installed in the MiG-31 are fundamentally similar to those employed by the MiG-25 derivative, referred to as the Ye-266M, which established a series of world height records.

MIKOYAN MIG-31 (FOXHOUND)

Dimensions: (Estimated) Span, 45 ft 9 in (13,94 m); length, 68 ft 10 in (21,00 m); height, 18 ft 6 in (5,63 m); wing area, 602·8 sq ft (56,00 m²).

NORMAN NAC 1 FREELANCE

Country of Origin: United Kingdom.

Type: Light cabin monoplane.

Power Plant: One 180 hp Avco Lycoming IO-360-A3A four-cylinder horizontally-opposed engine.

Performance: Max speed, 140 mph (225 km/h) at sea level; cruise (75% power), 135 mph (217 km/h) at sea level; max initial climb, 700 ft/min (3,6 m/sec); service ceiling, 17,000 ft (5 180 m); max range (no reserves and 75% power), 960 mls (1 545 km).

Weights: Empty equipped, 1,400 lb (613 kg); max take-off, 2,450 lb (1 114 kg).

Accommodation: Pilot and three passengers in side-by-side pairs of individual seats.

Status: Prototype first flown on 29 September 1984, with certification planned for spring 1986.

Notes: Built by NDN Aircraft for the Norman Aeroplane Company, the NAC 1 Freelance is a derivative of the BN-3 Nymph flown on 17 May 1969 (see 1970 edition), but has a more powerful engine, a new wing section, flaps and ailerons of different structure, increased fuel capacity of integral type, revised wing bracing, and various more minor improvements. Emphasis is placed by the Freelance on agricultural and utility tasks, a feature of the aeroplane being its aft-folding wings. These can be folded "within 30 seconds of engine shutdown" and allow the Freelance to be accommodated in a space 23 ft 6 in (7,16 m) long by 12 ft (3,66 m) wide. A 100 US gal (379 l) detachable spray tank with booms and nozzle or Micronair atomiser rigs may be attached beneath the fuselage, and skis or floats may be fitted.

NORMAN NAC 1 FREELANCE

Dimensions: Span, 39 ft 4 in (11,98 m); length, 23 ft 7¾ in (7,20 m); height, 9 ft 6 in (2,90 m); wing area, 169 sq ft (15,70 m²).

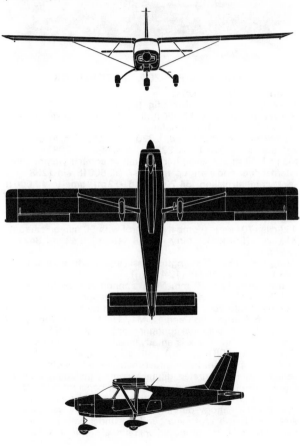

NORTHROP F-20A TIGERSHARK

Country of Origin: USA.
Type: Single-seat multi-role fighter.
Power Plant: One 17,000 lb st (7 711 kgp) reheat General Electric F404-GE-100 turbofan.
Performance: Max speed, 1,320 mph (2 124 km/h) or Mach 2·0 above 36,000 ft (10 975 m), 800 mph (1 288 km/h) or Mach 1·05 at sea level; initial climb at combat weight (50% internal fuel and wingtip missiles), 52,800 ft/min (268,2 m/sec); combat ceiling, 54,700 ft (16 672 m); time to 40,000 ft (12 190 m) from brakes release, 2·3 min; tactical radius with two 229 Imp gal/1 040 l drop tanks and 20 min reserve at sea level (HI-LO-HI interdiction with seven Mk 82 bombs), 437 mls (704 km), (combat air patrol with 96 min on station), 345 mls (555 km); ferry range (max fuel), 1,842 mls (2 965 km).
Weights: Take-off (wingtip missiles), 18,345 lb (8 321 kg); max take-off, 27,502 lb (12 475 kg).
Armament: Two 20-mm M-39 cannon and up to 7,000 lb (3 175 kg) of external ordnance on five stations.
Status: Prototypes of the F-20 were flown on 30 August 1982, 26 August 1983 and 12 May 1984, with fourth prototype (in fully operational configuration) to fly in 1986.
Notes: The Tigershark is an advanced derivative of the F-5E Tiger II (see 1981 edition) with a low-bypass turbofan affording 70 per cent more thrust than the twin engines of the earlier fighter, integrated digital avionics, including a digital flight control system, and a multi-mode coherent pulse-Doppler radar. The second and subsequent prototypes feature a new cockpit canopy offering 45 per cent more transparency area. The fourth prototype currently under construction will be completed in the proposed operational configuration.

NORTHROP F-20A TIGERSHARK

Dimensions: Span, 26 ft 8 in (8,13 m); length, 46 ft 6 in (14,17 m); height, 13 ft 10 in (4,22 m); wing area, 186 sq ft (17,28 m²).

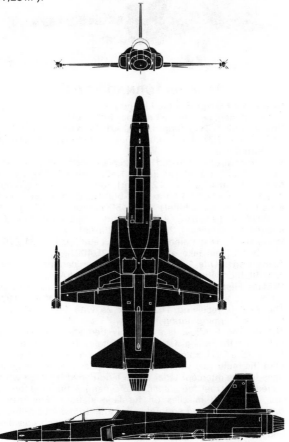

PANAVIA TORNADO F MK 2

Country of Origin: United Kingdom.
Type: Tandem two-seat air defence interceptor.
Power Plant: Two (approx) 9,000 lb st (4 082 kgp) dry and 17,000 lb st (7 711 kgp) reheat Turbo-Union RB199-34R Mk 104 turbofans.
Performance: (Estimated) Max speed, 920 mph (1 480 km/h) or Mach = 1·2 at sea level, 1,450 mph (2 333 km/h) or Mach = 2·2 at 40,000 ft (12 190 m); radius of action (combat air patrol with two 330 Imp gal/1 500 l drop tanks and allowance for two hours loiter), 350–450 mls (560–725 km); time to 30,000 ft (9 145 m), 1.7 min; ferry range (with four 330 Imp gal/1 500 l tanks), 2,650 mls (4 265 km).
Weights: (Estimated) Empty equipped, 31,970 lb (14 500 kg); max take-off, 56,000 lb (25 402 kg).
Armament: One 27-mm IWKA-Mauser cannon plus two AIM-9L Sidewinder and four BAe Sky Flash AAMs.
Status: First of three F Mk 2 prototypes flown on 27 October 1979, and first production aircraft flown on 5 March 1984. The RAF is receiving 162 F Mk 2s with first operational squadrons forming during 1985.
Notes: The F Mk 2 is a UK-only derivative of the multinational (UK, Federal Germany and Italy) Tornado multi-role fighter (see 1978 edition). Retaining 80 per cent commonality with the multi-role version, the F Mk 2 features a redesigned nose for the intercept radar and a lengthened fuselage which increases internal fuel capacity and permits the mounting of four Sky Flash missiles on fuselage stations. Emphasis is placed on range and endurance in order to mount combat air patrols at considerable distances from the British coastline, and a retractable flight refuelling probe is fitted.

162

PANAVIA TORNADO F MK 2

Dimensions: Span (25 deg sweep), 45 ft $7\frac{1}{4}$ in (13,90 m), (68 deg sweep), 28 ft $2\frac{1}{2}$ in (8,59 m); length, 59 ft 3 in (18,06 m); height, 18 ft $8\frac{1}{2}$ in (5,70 m); wing area, 322·9 sq ft (30,00 m²).

PARTENAVIA AP68 SPARTACUS

Country of Origin: Italy.
Type: Light multi-role transport, utility and (RG) coastal surveillance aircraft.
Power Plant: Two 330 shp Allison 250-B17C turboprops.
Performance: (AP68TP/300) Max cruising speed, 240 mph (386 km/h) at 15,000 ft (4 570 m); range cruise, 190 mph (306 km/h) at 12,000 ft (3 660 m); initial climb, 2,057 ft/min (10,45 m/sec); service ceiling, 25,000 ft (7 620 m); range (with 1,600-lb/726-kg payload), 378 mls (609 km) at max cruise, (with 820-lb/327-kg payload), 1,237 mls.
Weights: (AP68TP/300) Empty, 3,285 lb (1 490 kg); max take-off, 5,732 lb (2 600 kg).
Accommodation: Pilot and co-pilot/passenger in cockpit with three rows of paired individual seats in main cabin, the rearmost row being replaceable by a bench-type seat for three.
Status: The AP68TP/300 was flown on 29 March 1983 as the series version of the AP68TP/100 which entered flight test on 20 November 1981, and was, itself, derived from the AB68TP first flown on 11 September 1978. The RG (Retractable Gear) version was first flown in July 1984. Production of AP68TP/300 running at 1·5 monthly at beginning of 1985 and scheduled to rise to two-three monthly during year.
Notes: The Spartacus RG (illustrated) has been derived from the standard AP68TP/300 version of the Spartacus primarily to meet a requirement for a coastal surveillance aircraft. Apart from a retractable undercarriage, the Spartacus RG differs from the basic model in having an extended nose to accommodate radar. A further development, the AP68TC-RG/600, will have a 25·6-in (65-cm) stretch. A pressurised derivative with a larger cabin and a retractable undercarriage is under development as the Pulsar for certification in 1986–87.

PARTENAVIA AP68 SPARTACUS

Dimensions: Span, 39 ft 4½ in (12,00 m); length, 31 ft 9¾ in (9,70 m); height, 12 ft 0 in (3,65 m); wing area, 200·22 sq ft (18,60 m²).

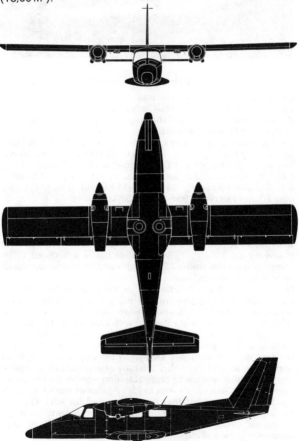

PILATUS PC-9

Country of Origin: Switzerland.

Type: Tandem two-seat basic/advanced trainer.

Power Plant: One 950 shp (flat-rated) Pratt & Whitney (Canada) PT6A-62 turboprop.

Perfoamance: Max speed, 308 mph (496 km/h) at sea level, 345 mph (556 km/h) at 20,000 ft (6 100 m); max cruise, 345 mph (556 km/h) at 18,000 ft (5 485 m); max initial climb, 4,000 ft/min (20,32 m/sec); time to 15,000 ft (4 575 m), 4·5 min; service ceiling, 38,000 ft (11 580 m); max range (5% plus 20 min reserves), 955 mls (1 538 km).

Weights: Basic empty, 3,570 lb (1 619 kg); empty equipped, 3,715 lb (1 685 kg); max take-off (clean), 4,960 lb (2 250 kg), (with external load), 7,055 lb (3 200 kg).

Status: First prototype flown on 7 May 1984, with second following on 20 July 1984. Certification is scheduled to be completed by December 1985, with initial customer deliveries early in the following year.

Notes: One of the competitors in the contest to meet the RAF's AST.412 requirement, the PC-9 bears a close external similarity to the PC-7 Turbo Trainer (see 1984 edition), but is, in fact, a very different design, with only about 10 per cent commonality of structure with the earlier trainer. Differences include a more powerful engine (flat-rated from 1,150 shp), the provision of vertically staggered ejection seats, modified wing profiles and tips, new ailerons and a ventral air brake. Under a memorandum of understanding signed on 15 March 1984, British Aerospace was to join Pilatus in manufacture of the PC-9 in the event that it was selected for AST.412, the British company being responsible for 85 per cent (in man-hours) of aircraft ordered by the RAF, with a 40 per cent production share of export aircraft.

PILATUS PC-9

Dimensions: Span, 33 ft 2½ in (10,12 m); length, 32 ft 11¾ in (10,05 m); height, 10 ft 8⅓ in (3,26 m); wing area, 175·3 sq ft (16,29 m²).

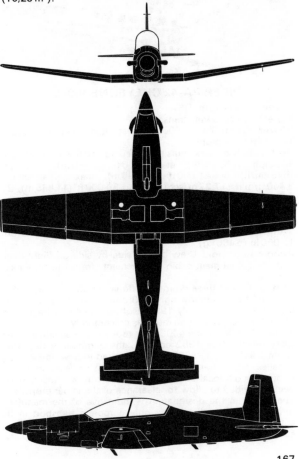

PIPER PA-42 CHEYENNE 400LS

Country of Origin: USA.

Type: Light corporate transport.

Power Plant: Two 1,000 shp (flat-rated) Garrett TPE331-14A/14B turboprops.

Performance: Max cruising speed (at 10,000 lb/4 536 kg), 405 mph (652 km/h) at 23,500 ft (7 165 m), 338 mph (545 km/h) at 41,000 ft (12 495 m); max initial climb, 3,400 ft/min (17,27 m/sec); time to 39,000 ft (11 885 m), 27 min; service ceiling 41,000 ft (12 495 m); range (six passengers), 1,340 mls (2 157 km) at 367 mph (591 km/h), (max fuel), 1,685 mls (2 711 km) at 370 mph (595 km/h).

Weights: Empty (typical), 7,546 lb (3 423 kg); max take-off, 12,050 lb (5 466 kg).

Accommodation: Crew of two side-by-side on flight deck and alternative main cabin arrangements for six to nine passengers.

Status: First of three prototypes flown on 23 February 1983, with certification following on 13 July 1984 and first customer delivery on 26 July 1984. Eight delivered by beginning of 1985 when production rate was one monthly.

Notes: The Cheyenne 400LS is a re-engined derivative of the Cheyenne III (see 1982 edition), the enormously flat-rated (from 1,645 shp) TPE331 being mounted in new, lower-drag nacelles, the airframe being entirely flush-riveted and embodying some local strengthening, and a new undercarriage being provided to allow for clearance of the larger propellers. The "400" in the designation is indicative of the manufacturer's claim that this is the only corporate transport in its category capable of achieving 400 mph (644 km/h), the "LS" suffix indicating Lear Siegler of which Piper is a subsidiary.

PIPER PA-42 CHEYENNE 400LS

Dimensions: Span, 47 ft 8½ in (14,53 m); length, 43 ft 4¾ in (13,23 m); height, 15 ft 6 in (4,72 m); wing area, 293 sq ft (27,20 m²).

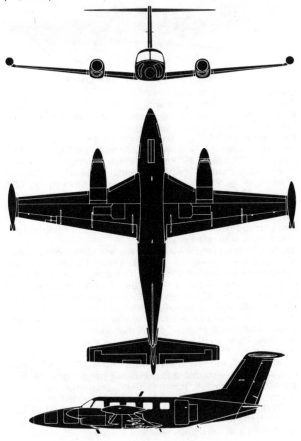

PIPER PA-46-310P MALIBU

Country of Origin: USA.

Type: Light cabin monoplane.

Power Plant: One 310 hp Continental TSIO-520-BE six-cylinder horizontally-opposed engine.

Performance: Max speed, 254 mph (409 km/h) at optimum altitude; cruise (75% power), 239 mph (385 km/h), 65% power), 225 mph (363 km/h); initial climb, 1,143 ft/min (5,8 m/sec); range (with 45 min reserves), 1,542 mls (2 482 km) at 75% power, 1,657 mls (2 667 km) at 65% power, 1,830 mls (2 945 km) at 55% power.

Weights: Standard empty, 2,275 lb (1 032 kg); max take-off, 3,850 lb (1 746 kg).

Accommodation: Pilot and five passengers in paired individual seats with rear airstair door.

Status: First prototype Malibu flown late 1980, with production prototype flying in August 1982. Certification was obtained in September 1983, with customer deliveries commencing in the following November. One hundred delivered by beginning of 1985 when production rate was 10 monthly.

Notes: Intended to compete with the Cessna P210 Centurion, which, prior to the advent of the Malibu, was the sole pressurised single-engined cabin monoplane on the market, this new Piper aircraft is claimed to be the first production single-engined general aviation model to utilise computer-aided design and manufacturing (CAD/CAM) techniques. Possessing no relationship to previous Piper designs, the Malibu offers a cabin of "business twin" proportions with club seating and a rear airstair door, and is designed to give an 8,000 ft (2 440 m) cabin pressure up to 25,000 ft (7 620 m), at which the intercooling techniques of the TSIO-520 engine result in 240 hp still being available.

PIPER PA-46-310P MALIBU

Dimensions: Span, 43 ft 0 in (13,10 m); length, 28 ft 4¾ in (8,66 m); height, 11 ft 3½ in (3,44 m); wing area, 175 sq ft (16,26 m²).

PZL-130 ORLIK

Country of Origin: Poland.
Type: Tandem two-seat primary/basic trainer.
Power Plant: One 300 hp PZL (Ivchenko) AI-14R nine-cylinder radial air-cooled engine.
Performance: Max speed, 236 mph (380 km/h); max continuous cruise, 205 mph (330 km/h); max initial climb, 1,460 ft/min (7,4 m/sec); service ceiling, 22,965 ft (7 000 m); max range, 910 mls (1 460 km).
Weights: Empty, 2,094 lb (950 kg); normal loaded, 2,866 lb (1 300 kg); max take-off, 3,310 lb (1 500 kg).
Status: First of two prototypes flown on 12 October 1984. Evaluation being conducted by Polish Air Force during 1985, with, if selected, production scheduled to commence in 1986.
Notes: The Orlik (Eaglet) is one of two types of primary/basic trainer currently being evaluated for production for the Polish Air Force, the other being the M-26 Iskierka (Little Spark). Described as a "pre-jet" trainer, being intended to carry the pupil from *ab initio* instruction through conversion to a jet trainer, such as the TS-11 Iskra, the Orlik is being proposed with various standards of avionics up to IFR instruction and with wing hardpoints to allow for external light ordnance loads to be carried for the weapons training task. Fully aerobatic, the Orlik is said to simulate many of the low-speed characteristics of heavier and faster pure jet aircraft, and its cockpit layout resembles that of an operational aircraft. The three-bladed propeller is unusual in being of fixed-pitch type, and a turboprop-powered derivative of the Orlik is reportedly proposed.

PZL-130 ORLIK

Dimensions: Span, 26 ft 3 in (8,00 m); length, 27 ft 9 in (8,45 m); height, 13 ft 1½ in (4,00 m); wing area, 131·3 sq ft (12,20 m²).

RHEIN-FLUGZEUGBAU FANTRAINER

Country of Origin: Federal Germany.
Type: Tandem two-seat primary/basic trainer.
Power Plant: One (Fantrainer 400) 420 shp Allison 250-C20B or (Fantrainer 600) 600 shp Allison 250-C30 turbo-shaft driving a five-bladed ducted fan.
Performance: (Fantrainer 400) Max speed, 230 mph (370 km/h) at 10,000 ft (3 050 m); initial climb, 2,000 ft/min (10,2 m/sec); range (no reserves), 1,094 mls (1 760 km). (Fantrainer 600) Max speed, 267 mph (430 km/h) at 18,000 ft (5 485 m); initial climb, 3,150 ft/min (16 m/sec); range (no reserves), 863 mls (1 390 km).
Weights: (Fantrainer 400) Empty, 2,456 lb (1 114 kg); max take-off, 3,968 lb (1 800 kg). (Fantrainer 600) Empty 2,557 lb (1 160 kg); max take-off, 5,071 lb (2 300 kg).
Status: First of two prototypes flown 27 October 1977, and first production aircraft (Fantrainer 600) flown on 12 August 1984. The Royal Thai Air Force has ordered 31 Fantrainer 400s and 16 Fantrainer 600s, and has an option on a further 26 Fantrainer 600s, deliveries to Thailand having commenced in October 1984. Production was increasing from one to 2·5 monthly at the beginning of 1985.
Notes: First two aircraft for Thailand shipped in flyaway condition and remainder being supplied as major component kits for assembly in Thailand with locally-manufactured wings, the workshare between RFB and Thailand progressively increasing from a ratio of 80:20 to 57:43. Of unconventional design, the Fantrainer minimises transition problems by simulating pure jet flight.

RHEIN-FLUGZEUGBAU FANTRAINER

Dimensions: Span, 31 ft 10 in (9,70 m); length, 30 ft 3½ in (9,23 m); height, 9 ft 10 in (3,00 m); wing area, 149·6 sq ft (13,90 m²).

ROCKWELL B-1B

Country of Origin: USA.
Type: Strategic bomber and cruise missile carrier.
Power Plant: Four 30,750 lb st (13 948 kgp) General Electric F101-GE-102 turbofans.
Performance: Max speed (clean condition), 792 mph (1 275 km/h) or Mach = 1·2 at 40,000 ft (12 190 m); low-level penetration speed, 610 mph (980 km/h) or Mach = 0·8.
Weights: Empty, 179,985 lb (81 641 kg); max take-off, 477,000 lb (216 367 kg).
Accommodation: Flight crew of four comprising pilot, co-pilot and offensive and defensive systems operators.
Armament: Eight AGM-86B cruise missiles and 12 AGM-69 defence-suppression missiles internally, plus 12–14 AGM-86Bs externally, or 84 500-lb (227-kg) Mk 82 bombs internally, plus 44 externally, or 24 free-falling B-61 nuclear bombs, plus 14 externally.
Status: First contract placed 20 January 1982 in programme entailing manufacture of 100 B-1Bs, the first having flown on 18 October 1984. Fifteenth B-1B to be delivered mid-1986, with production attaining four monthly by late 1986 and 100th delivered by April 1988.
Notes: The B-1B is a derivative of the Mach 2·2 B-1, first of four prototypes of which flew 23 December 1974. A 347-flight, 1,895-hour test programme was completed with these aircraft on 30 April 1981. The B-1B has a reduced speed capability by comparison with the B-1, being optimised for low-level penetration. After modification to incorporate many of the B-1B features, the second B-1 prototype resumed flight testing on 23 March 1983, and was joined in July 1984 by the fourth B-1 prototype which incorporates the remainder of the B-1B features. Initial operational capability is expected to be attained in 1986, and each USAF squadron will have sixteen B-1Bs plus supporting tankers.

ROCKWELL B-1B

Dimensions: Span (15 deg), 136 ft 8½ in (41,67 m), (67·5 deg), 78 ft 2½ in (23,84 m); length, 146 ft 8 in (44,70 m); height, 33 ft 7¼ in (10,24 m); wing area (approx), 1,950 sq ft (181,2 m²).

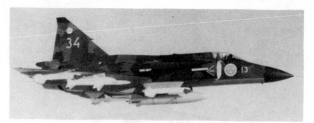

SAAB (JA) 37 VIGGEN

Country of Origin: Sweden.
Type: Single-seat all-weather interceptor fighter with secondary strike capability.
Power Plant: One 16,200 lb st (7 350 kgp) dry and 28,110 lb st (12 750 kgp) reheat Volvo Flygmotor RM 8B turbofan.
Performance: Max speed (with four AAMs), 838 mph (1 350 km/h) or Mach 1·1 at sea level, 1,255–1,365 mph (2 020–2 195 km/h) or Mach 1·9–2·1 at 36,090 ft (11 000 m); time (from brakes off) to 32,810 ft (10 000 m), 1·4 min; tactical radius (Mach 2·0 intercept mission), 250 mls (400 km), (counterair mission with centreline drop tank and 3,000 lb/ 1 360 kg of external ordnance), 650 mls (1 046 km) HI-LO-HI, 300 mls (480 km) LO-LO-LO.
Weights: Empty (approx), 26,895 lb (12 200 kg); combat (cannon armament and half fuel), 33,070 lb (15 000 kg), (with four AAMs), 37,040 lb (16 800 kg); max take-off, 49,600 lb (22 500 kg).
Armament: One 30-mm Oerlikon KCA cannon and (intercept) two Rb 72 Sky Flash and two (or four) Rb 24 Sidewinder AAMs, or (interdiction) 13,227 lb (6 000 kg) of ordnance.
Status: First of four JA 37 prototypes (modified from AJ 37 airframes) flown June 1974, with fifth and definitive prototype flown 15 December 1975. First production JA 37 flown on 4 November 1977, and total of 149 JA 37s (of 329 Viggens of all types) being produced for Swedish Air Force with some 110 delivered by beginning of 1985 and final deliveries scheduled for 1986.
Notes: The JA 37 is an optimised interceptor derivative of the AJ 37 attack aircraft (see 1973 edition), and will eventually equip eight squadrons of the Swedish Air Force.

SAAB (JA) 37 VIGGEN

Dimensions: Span, 34 ft 9¼ in (10,60 m); length (excluding probe) 50 ft 8¼ in (15,45 m); height, 19 ft 4¼ in (5,90 m); wing area (including foreplanes), 561·88 sq ft (52,20 m²).

SAAB-FAIRCHILD 340

Countries of Origin: Sweden and USA.
Type: Regional airliner and corporate transport.
Power Plant: Two 1,700 shp General Electric CT7-5A-1 or (corporate version) 1,600 shp CT7-7E turboprops.
Performance: (Regional airliner) Max cruising speed, 315 mph (508 km/h) at 15,000 ft (4570 m); econ cruise, 290 mph (467 km/h) at 25,000 ft (7620 m); max initial climb, 1,7650 ft/min (8,94 m/sec); range (max passengers with reserves) 920 mls (1480 km).
Weights: Operational empty (typical), 17,000 lb (7711 kg); max take-off, 12,247 lb (27000 kg).
Accommodation: Flight crew of two and standard regional airliner arrangement for 35 passengers three abreast with offset aisle. Standard corporate transport arrangement provides 16 seats with various options.
Status: First of three prototypes flown 25 January 1983, and first production example flown on 5 March 1984. Entered commercial service (with Crossair) on 15 June 1984, and firm orders placed for 77 aircraft by beginning of 1985.
Notes: The Saab-Fairchild 340 is being manufactured under a joint programme between Saab-Scania (Sweden) and Fairchild (USA), with development costs shared 65–35 between the Swedish and US partners. Manufacture of the fuselage and final assembly is undertaken by Saab-Scania, the wing, tail surfaces and engine nacelles being produced by Fairchild. Deliveries of the corporate transport version were expected to commence early 1985, and winglets, tested during 1984 on the first prototype, may be offered as an option.

SAAB-FAIRCHILD 340

Dimensions: Span, 70 ft 4 in (21,44 m); length, 64 ft 9 in (19,72 m); height, 22 ft 6 in (6,87 m); wing area, 450 sq ft (41,81 m²).

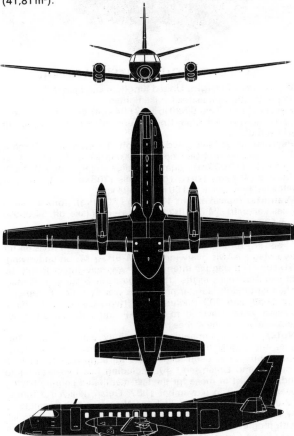

SEPECAT JAGUAR INTERNATIONAL

Countries of Origin: United Kingdom and France.
Type: Single-seat tactical strike fighter.
Power Plant: Two 5,520 lb st (2 504 kgp) dry and 8,400 lb st (3 811 kgp) reheat Rolls-Royce/Turboméca RT172-58 Adour 811 turbofans.
Performance: Max speed, 820 mph (1 320 km/h) or Mach = 1·1 at sea level, 1,057 mph (1 700 km/h) or Mach = 1·6 at 32,810 ft (10 000 m); combat radius (with external fuel), 282 mls (454 km) LO-LO-LO, 440 mls (708 km) HI-LO-HI; unrefuelled ferry range, 2,190 mls (3 524 km).
Weights: Typical empty, 15,432 lb (7 000 kg); normal loaded (clean aircraft), 24,000 lb (11 000 kg); max take-off, 34,000 lb (15 422 kg).
Armament: Two 30-mm Aden cannon and up to 10,000 lb (4 536 kg) of ordnance on five external stations. Provision for two Magic AAMs overwing or AIM-9P AAMs on underwing.
Status: The Jaguar International was developed jointly by British Aerospace in the UK and Dassault-Breguet in France. The first of eight Jaguar prototypes was flown on 8 September 1968, and 202 (including 37 two-seaters) of the basic version were delivered to the RAF and 200 (including 40 two-seaters) to the *Armée de l'Air*.
Notes: Although manufactured jointly with Dassault-Breguet, the Jaguar International is assembled by British Aerospace which has been responsible for supplying 12 each to Ecuador and Oman, and 40 (including five two-seaters) to India, the last of those for the last-mentioned country having been delivered in November 1982. Oman received a further 12 during 1983, delivery of 18 to Nigeria is to be completed by mid-1985, and 76 are being assembled by HAL in India, with progressive component manufacture, 12 of these having been flown by the beginning of 1985.

SEPECAT JAGUAR INTERNATIONAL

Dimensions: Span, 28 ft 6 in (8,69 m); length, 50 ft 11 in (15,52 m); height, 16 ft 0½ in (4,89 m); wing area, 280·3 sq ft (24,18 m²).

SHORTS C-23A (SHERPA)

Country of Origin: United Kingdom.
Type: Light military utility transport.
Power Plant: Two 1,198 shp Pratt & Whitney (Canada) PT6A-45R turboprops.
Performance: Max cruising speed (at 21,000 lb/9 525 kg), 218 mph (352 km/h) at 10,000 ft (3 050 m); econ cruise, 181 mph (291 km/h) at 10,000 ft (3 050 m); max initial climb, 1,180 ft/min (6,0 m/sec); range with reserves for 45-min hold and 50-mile (80-km diversion (with 7,000-lb/3 175-kg payload), 225 mls (362 km), (with 5,000-lb/2 268-kg payload), 770 mls (1 239 km).
Weights: Operational empty (typical), 14,200 lb (6 440 kg); max take-off, 22,900 lb (10 387 kg).
Accommodation: Flight crew of three and typical loads of nine passengers and two LD3 freight containers, four LD3 or seven CO8 containers, or two half-ton vehicles.
Status: Prototype Sherpa flown on 23 December 1982, and order for 18 placed (plus an option taken on a further 48) by USAF on 2 March 1984 as C-23A. First C-23A flown 6 August 1984, and three delivered by beginning of 1985, with remaining 15 of initial order scheduled for delivery by August 1985.
Notes: The Sherpa is a freighter version of the Shorts 330-200 30-passenger regional airlines (see 1983 edition), the C-23A version for the USAF having most cabin windows deleted. The Sherpa has a rear loading ramp and a roller conveyor system. The Shorts 330-UTT (utility tactical transport) has twin side-loading doors rather than the rear ramp and has been ordered by the Thai Army and Thai Royal Border Patrol Police.

SHORTS C-23A (SHERPA)

Dimensions: Span, 74 ft 9 in (22,78 m); length, 58 ft 0 in (17,69 m); height, 16 ft 3 in (4,95 m); wing area, 453 sq ft (42,10 m²).

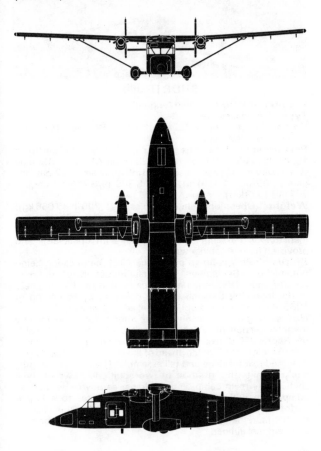

SHORTS 360

Country of Origin: United Kingdom.

Type: Regional airliner.

Power Plant: Two 1,327 shp Pratt & Whitney (Canada) PT6A-65R turboprops.

Performance: Max cruising speed, 244 mph (393 km/h) at 10,000 ft (3 050 m); econ cruise, 230 mph (370 km/h); range with reserves (36 passengers), 345 mls (556 km), (27 passengers), 795 mls (1 280 km), (with 8,300-lb/3 765-kg cargo), 207 mls (333 km).

Weights: Operational empty (typical), 16,900 lb (7 666 kg); max take-off, 26,000 lb (11 794 kg).

Accommodation: Flight crew of two with standard arrangement for 36 passengers three abreast with offset aisle and provision for one cabin attendant.

Status: Prototype flown on 1 June 1981, certification being obtained on 3 September 1982. First production aircraft flown on 19 August 1982, entering service (with Suburban Airlines) in the following December. Sixty delivered by beginning of 1985, when orders and options totalled 100 aircraft.

Notes: A growth version of the Shorts 330 (the military freighter version of which is described on pages 184–185), the Shorts 360 differs from its progenitor primarily in having a 3-ft (91-cm) cabin stretch ahead of the wing and an entirely redesigned rear fuselage and tail assembly. The fuselage lengthening permits the insertion of two additional rows of three seats in the main cabin, and the lower aerodynamic drag by comparison with the earlier aircraft contributes to a higher performance. The Shorts 360 is unpressurised and is claimed to offer more baggage space per passenger than any comparable regional airliner.

SHORTS 360

Dimensions: 74 ft 10 in (22,81 m); length, 70 ft 10 in (21,59 m); height, 23 ft 8 in (7,21 m); wing area, 454 sq ft (42,18 m²).

SIAI MARCHETTI SF 600TP CANGURO

Country of Origin: Italy.
Type: Light utility transport.
Power Plant: Two 429 shp Allison 250-B17C turboprops.
Performance: (Fixed undercarriage) Max cruising speed, 190 mph (306 km/h) at 5,000 ft (1 525 m); cruise (75% power), 178 mph (287 km/h) at 10,000 ft (3 050 m); max initial climb, 1,515 ft-min (7,7 m/sec); service ceiling, 24,000 ft (7 315 m); range (max payload), 372 mls (600 km), (max internal fuel), 981 mls (1 580 km), (plus two 66 Imp gal/300 l external auxiliary tanks), 1,398 mls (2 250 km).
Weights: (Fixed undercarriage) Empty equipped (freight), 3,968 lb (1 800 kg); max take-off, 7,275 lb (3 300 kg), (with external fuel), 8,157 lb (3 700 kg).
Accommodation: Pilot and co-pilot/passenger on flight deck and provision for up to nine passengers in main cabin. Optional internal arrangements for six passengers in corporate transport version, four stretcher patients and two medical attendants in aeromedical version, and 12 paratroops in military transport version.
Status: Derived from the piston-engined F 600 Canguro, the SF 600TP (the original prototype re-engined) flew on 8 April 1981. The third prototype (with retractable undercarriage) entered flight test in August 1984, and work was proceeding on a further prototype and six production aircraft at the beginning of 1985.
Notes: Available with both fixed and retractable undercarriages, and with a side-hinged rear fuselage for direct freight loading, the Canguro (Kangaroo) is proposed in a variety of versions, with tasks ranging from maritime surveillance and electronic intelligence to crop spraying and dusting.

SIAI MARCHETTI SF 600TP CANGURO

Dimensions: Span, 49 ft 2½ in (15,00 m); length, 39 ft 10½ in (12,15 m); height, 15 ft 1 in (4,60 m); wing area, 258·3 sq ft (24,00 m²).

SIAI MARCHETTI S.211

Country of Origin: Italy.

Type: Tandem two-seat basic trainer.

Power Plant: One 2,500 lb st (1 134 kgp) Pratt & Whitney (Canada) JT15D-4C turbofan.

Performance: Max speed, 420 mph (676 km/h) at 25,000 ft (7 620 m); max cruise, 414 mph (667 km/h) at 25,000 ft (7 620 m); max initial climb, 4,200 ft/min (21,34 m/sec); service ceiling, 40,000 ft (12 200 m); ferry range (with two 77 Imp gal/350 l external tanks), 1,543 mls (2 483 km).

Weights: Empty equipped, 3,560 lb (1 615 kg); loaded (training mission), 5,842 lb (2 650 kg); max take-off, 6,834 lb (3 100 kg).

Armament: Max external load of 1,320 lb (600 kg) may be carried by four wing pylons. This may comprise four single- or twin-gun 7,62-mm or four 12,7-mm pods, or two 20-mm gun pods, four bombs of up to 330 lb (150 kg) weight or two of up to 661 lb (300 kg) weight, various rocket pods, or combinations of these.

Status: First of three prototypes flown on 10 April 1981, and first production example (for Singapore) flown on 4 October 1984. Initial production contract from Singapore calls for 10 aircraft of which first six completed in Italy (disassembled after testing and reassembled in Singapore) and remaining four supplied as complete kits. A further 20 (for supply in partial kit form) are on option.

Notes: Developed by the Siai Marchetti subsidiary of the Agusta group as a private venture, the S.211 represents an attempt to arrest the upward spiralling cost of training military pilots. Less than half the empty weight of other new-generation jet trainers, the S.211 is lighter than such turboprop trainers as the EMB-312 Tucano. It is, nevertheless, comparatively sophisticated and features a supercritical wing.

SIAI MARCHETTI S.211

Dimensions: Span, 27 ft 8 in (8,43 m); length, 31 ft 2⅔ in (9,50 m); height, 12 ft 5½ in (3,80 m); wing area, 135·63 sq ft (12,60 m²).

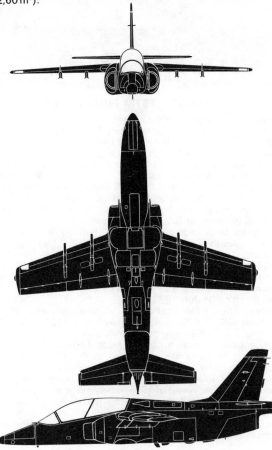

SLINGSBY T67M FIREFLY 160

Country of Origin: United Kingdom.
Type: Side-by-side two-seat primary/basic trainer.
Power Plant: One 160 hp Avco Lycoming AEIO-320-D1B four-cylinder horizontally-opposed engine.
Performance: (At max take-off weight) Max speed, 159 mph (256 km/h) at sea level; max cruise (75% power), 144 mph (231 km/h) at 8,000 ft (2 440 m); max initial climb, 1,180 ft/min (5,99 m/sec); service ceiling, 15,000 ft (4 570 m); range (max fuel and 45 min reserve at 45% power), 420 mls (676 km) at 75% power.
Weights: Empty equipped, 1,410 lb (640 kg); loaded (aerobatic), 1,950 lb (884 kg); max take-off, 2,000 lb (907 kg).
Status: The T67M prototype was flown on 5 December 1982, certification being attained in September 1983, and initial customer deliveries (to Specialist Flying Training) commencing shortly afterwards. The first production T67M was flown on 31 July 1983.
Notes: The T67M Firefly is a military derivative of the primarily-GRF T-67B, which, powered by a 116 hp Avco Lycoming O-235-N2A engine, is itself a derivative of the T67 (a licence-built version of the French Fournier RF6B). The T67C and D are similarly powered to the T67M and have fixed-pitch and constant-speed propellers respectively. Twenty GRP (glass-reinforced plastics) T67s had been completed by the beginning of 1985, when it was anticipated that 16 would be manufactured during the course of the year when progress would be made towards an "ideal" rate of 35 aircraft annually. The T67M differs structurally from other versions only in having spin strakes added.

SLINGSBY T67M FIREFLY 160

Dimensions: Span, 34 ft 9 in (10,59 m); length, 23 ft 0 in (7,01 m); height, 8 ft 3 in (2,51 m); wing area, 136.0 sq ft (12,63 m²).

SOKO (CNAIR IAR-93B) ORAO 2

Countries of Origin: Yugoslavia and Romania.

Type: Single-seat close air support fighter.

Power Plant: Two 3,880 lb st (1 760 kgp) dry and 5,000 lb st (2 268 kgp) reheat Orao- (or Turbomecanica-) built Rolls-Royce Viper 633-41 turbojets.

Performance: Max speed (at 18,629 lb/8 450 kg), 721 mph (1 160 km/h) of Mach = 0·946 at sea level, 634 mph (1 020 km/h) at 36,090 ft (11 000 m) or Mach = 0·96; max cruise, 449 mph (723 km/h) at 22,965 ft (7 000 m); max initial climb, 13,780 ft/min (70 m/sec); service ceiling, 44,300 ft (13 500 m); tactical radius (LO-LO-LO with four rocket pods), 162 mls (260 km), (LO-LO-HI with one 110 Imp gal/500 l drop tank and four 550-lb/250-kg bombs), 280 mls (450 km) with five min loiter.

Weights: Empty equipped, 12,676 lb (5 750 kg); basic operational, 18,629 lb (8 450 kg); max take-off, 24,800 lb (11 250 kg).

Armament: Two 23-mm twin-barrel GSh-23L cannon and max external ordnance load of 3,615 lb (1 640 kg) distributed between one fuselage and four wing stations.

Status: Two prototypes flown 31 October 1974 (one in Yugoslavia and one in Romania) of Orao 1 (IAR-93A), with prototypes of the Orao 2 (IAR-93B) following during last quarter of 1983, the latter being the production version at the beginning of 1985.

Notes: The Orao (Eagle) has been developed as a joint programme between SOKO in Yugoslavia and CNIAR in Romania, with final assembly lines in both countries. The Orao 1 (IAR-93A) differs primarily in having unreheated engines.

194

SOKO (CNIAR IAR-93B) ORAO 2

Dimensions: Span, 31 ft 6¾ in (9,62 m); length (excluding probe), 48 ft 10⅔ in (14,90 m); height, 14 ft 9⅛ in (4,50 m); wing area, 279·87 sq ft (26,00 m²).

SOKO GALEB 4

Country of Origin: Yugoslavia.

Type: Tandem two-seat basic and advanced trainer and light strike aricraft.

Power Plant: One 4,000 lb st (1 814 kgp) Rolls-Royce Viper 632-48 turbojet.

Performance: (At 10,494 lb/4 760 kg) Max speed, 565 mph (910 km/h) at 19,685 ft (6 000 m); max climb, 5,905 ft/min (30 m/sec); time to 26,245 ft (8 000 m), 6·0 min; combat radius (at 11,442 lb/5 190 kg) with ventral gun pack and two rocket pods, 186 mls (300 km) LO-LO-LO.

Weights: Empty equipped, 7,165 lb (3 250 kg); normal loaded (training mission), 10,494 lb (4 760 kg), (combat mission), 13,470 lb (6 110 kg); max overload, 13,955 lb (6 330 kg).

Armament: One 23-mm twin-barrel GSh-23L cannon in ventral pack and various external ordnance loads on four external hardpoints of 772 lb (350 kg) capacity inboard and 551 lb (250 kg) outboard.

Status: First of two prototypes flown on 17 July 1978 with second following on 18 December 1979. First of pre-series batch flown on 17 December 1980, with series production version entering Yugoslav Air Force service early 1983.

Notes: The G-4 Super Galeb (Super Gull) has been developed as a successor in Yugoslav Air Force service to the G-2A Galeb, but possessing no commonality with its predecessor other than design origin. Pre-series aircraft differed from the production model illustrated in having a conventional tail with neither dihedral nor anhedral, this being supplanted by an all-flying anhedralled tail. At the beginning of 1985, reheated and single-seat strike variants were being studied.

SOKO GALEB 4

Dimensions: Span, 32 ft 5 in (9,88 m); length, 38 ft 11 in (11,86 m); height, 14 ft 0 in (4,28 m); wing area, 209·9 sq ft (19,50 m²).

SUKHOI SU-22 (FITTER)

Country of Origin: USSR.

Type: Single-seat counterair and attack aircraft.

Power Plant: One 17,635 lb st (8 000 kgp) dry and 25,350 lb st (11 500 kgp) reheat Tumansky R-29B turbojet.

Performance: (Estimated for Su-22BM) Max speed (clean aircraft with 60% fuel), 1,430 mph (2 300 km/h) at 39,370 ft (12 000 m), or Mach = 2·17, 808 mph (1 300 km/h) at sea level, or Mach = 1·06; max initial climb, 44,290 ft/min (225 m/sec); combat radius (with 4,410 lb/2 000 kg external stores including drop tanks on outboard wing pylons), 320 mls (515 km) LO-LO-LO, 480 mls (770 km) HI-LO-HI.

Weights: (Estimated) Empty equipped, 22,045 lb (10 000 kg); max take-off, 39,022 lb (17 700 kg).

Armament: Two 30-mm NR-30 cannon and max external ordnance load of 7,716 lb (3 500 kg) distributed between ten (four fuselage and six wing) pylons.

Status: The Su-22 appeared in service in 1979 as a re-engined Su-20M. The Su-20 was, itself, fundamentally a re-engined Su-17, the former entering service in 1976 and the latter in 1981. Between 800 and 900 (all versions) are currently serving with the Soviet Air Force and Naval Aviation.

Notes: Differing from the Su-20 (Lyulka AL-21F turbojet) promarily in the type of engine installed, the Su-22 has been built in a number of versions. The principal of these are the Fitter-H (Su 22BM) illustrated above, the Fitter-J and the Fitter-K (illustrated on opposite page). The Fitter-J has been exported to eight countries.

SUKHOI SU-22 (FITTER)

Dimensions: (Estimated) Span (28 deg sweep), 45 ft 0 in (13,70 m), (68 deg sweep), 32 ft 6 in (9,90 m); length (including probe) 58 ft 3 in (17,75 m); height, 15 ft 5 in (4,70 m); wing area, 410 sq ft (38,00 m²).

SUKHOI SU-24 (FENCER)

Country of Origin: USSR.

Type: Deep penetration interdictor and strike aircraft.

Power Plant: Two (approx) 16,975 lb st (7 000 kgp) dry and 24,250 lb st (11 000 kgp) reheat Lyulka turbojets.

Performance: (Estimated) Max speed (clean), 915 mph (1 470 km/h) or Mach = 1·2 at sea level, 1,520 mph (2 446 km/h) or Mach = 2·3 above 36,000 ft (11 000 m); tactical radius (combat tanks and 4,400 lb/2 000 kg ordnance), 345 mls (555 km) LO-LO-LO, 1,050 mls (1 690 km) HI-LO-HI.

Weights: (Estimated) Empty equipped, 41,890 lb (19 000 kg); max take-off, 87,080 lb (39 500 kg).

Armament: One 23-mm or 30-mm rotary cannon (port side of fuselage) and eight (four wing and four fuselage) hardpoints for up to 17,635 lb (8 000 kg) of ordnance.

Status: Prototype believed flown 1970, with initial operational status achieved late 1974. Total of 450–500 in service at beginning of 1985 with both Frontal and Strategic Aviation elements of the Soviet Air Forces, those assigned to the latter being expected to increase by some 50 per cent by 1987–88.

Notes: The first Soviet aircraft designed from the outset for interdiction and counterair missions, the Su-24 carries pilot and weapon systems operator side by side, and is equipped with terrain avoidance radar. The initial service versions were referred to by NATO as the Fencer-A and -B, the later Fencer-C being illustrated. Whereas the A and B versions differed essentially in configuration of the rear fuselage box around the jet nozzles, the Fencer-C introduced important equipment changes indicated by new fairings, auxiliary intakes and probes. Production of the Fencer is believed to be continuing at a rate of 8–10 monthly.

SUKHOI SU-24 (FENCER)

Dimensions: (Estimated) Span (16 deg sweep), 56 ft 6 in (17.25 m), (68 deg sweep), 33 ft 9 in (10,30 m); length (excluding probes), 65 ft 6 in (20,00 m); height, 18 ft 0 in (5,50 m); wing area, 452 sq ft (42,00 m²).

SUKHOI SU-25 (FROGFOOT)

Country of Origin: USSR.
Type: Single-seat attack and close air support aircraft.
Power Plant: Two 11,240 lb st (5 100 kgp) Tumansky R-13-300 turbojets.
Performance: (Estimated) Max speed, 520 mph (837 km/h) at 10,000 ft (3 050 m); combat radius (with podded cannon and approx 8,000 lb/3 630 kg external ordnance, close air support mission LO-LO-LO), 300 mls (485 km) plus 1 hr loiter.
Weights: (Estimated) Max take-off, 37,000 lb (16 785 kg).
Armament: One heavy calibre gun (believed six-barrel 30-mm rotary cannon) beneath centre fuselage and up to 8,000 lb (3 630 kg) ordnance distributed between 10 (eight wing and two fuselage) external stores stations.
Status: First observed under test in the late 'seventies, prototypes presumably having flown in 1977–78, with initial deliveries to the Soviet Air Force following in 1980–81. Full operational capability was apparently achieved in 1983–84, and production was continuing at Tbilisi at the beginning of 1985 when 80–90 were believed in service with the Soviet Air Force and others with the Czechoslovak Air Force.
Notes: The Soviet equivalent of the USAF's Fairchild A-10A Thunderbolt II (see 1982 edition), the Su-25 has been in continuous service in Afghanistan since first being deployed to that country with an operational trials unit in 1981. The Su-25 features airbrakes at the rear of the wingtip pods and has anti-missile flare dispensers in the rear fuselage. During operations in Afghanistan it has apparently been used to perfect low-level tactics in co-ordination with Mi-24 gunship helicopters.

SUKHOI SU-25 (FROGFOOT)

Dimensions: (Estimated) Span, 53 ft 0 in (16,15 m); length (without nose and tail probes), 54 ft 0 in (16,46 m), (including probes), 58 ft 0 in (17,68 m); height, 17 ft 0 in (5,18 m).

SUKHOI SU-26

Country of Origin: USSR.
Type: Single-seat aerobatic competition aircraft.
Power Plant: One 360 hp Vedeneev M-14P nine-cylinder radial air-cooled engine.
Performance: Max speed, 205 mph (330 km/h); manoeuvering speed, 200 mph (320 km/h); normal cruise, 192 mph (310 km/h); range at normal cruise, 311 mls (500 km).
Weights: Normal competition take-off, (approx) 1 984 lb (900 kg).
Status: First of several prototypes flown late June 1984, and development continuing at the beginning of 1985.
Notes: Designed specifically for aerobatic flying and in a similar category to the Yak-55 (see 1983 edition), the Su-26 was developed by a team led by Vyacheslav Kondratiev to a requirement of the Central Committee of the para-military DOSAAF organisation (the aeronautical branch of which controls all sports flying in the Soviet Union). The first example was completed within 10 months of the initiation of design. The Su-26 makes extensive use of carbonfibre and glassfibre in its construction, the wing comprising two carbonfibre spars and triple-layer glassfibre panels with a phonoplastic filling and the fuselage being of welded steel tube construction with fibreglass skinning. The pilot's seat may be reclined 45 deg to increase resistance to *g* and the aircraft is stressed to + 11 and −9 *g* limits. The Su-26 is claimed to be the world's first aerobatic aircraft to make extensive use of plastics in its construction, and two examples participated in the World Aerobatic Championships held in Hungary 13–27 August 1984.

SUKHOI SU-26

Dimensions: Span, 25 ft 7 in (7,80 m); length, 22 ft 3¾ in (6,80 m); wing area, 128·09 sq ft (11,90 m²).

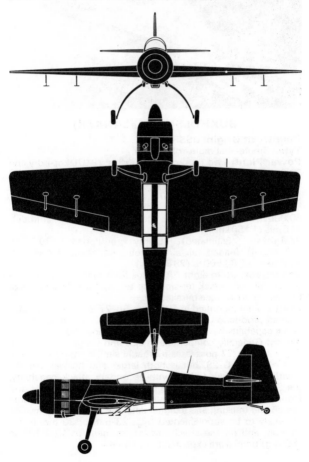

SUKHOI SU-27 (FLANKER)

Country of Origin: USSR.
Type: Single-seat multi-role fighter.
Power Plant: Two (approx) 20,000 lb st (9 070 kgp) dry and 30,000 lb st (13 610 kgp) reheat unidentified turbofans.
Performance: (Estimated) Max speed, 1,520 mph (1,445 km/h) above 36,100 ft (11 000 m) or Mach = 2·3, 835 mph (1 345 km/h) at sea level or Mach = 1·1; initial climb, 60,000 ft/min (304,5 m/sec); tactical radius (high altitude). 715 mls (1 150 km).
Weights: (Estimated) Empty equipped, 39,000 lb (17 690 kg); loaded (air-air mission), 44,000 lb (19 960 kg); max take-off, 63,500 lb (28 805 kg).
Armament: Up to eight AA-10 medium-range AAMs for the air-air role, or (attack mission) up to 13,200 lb (5 990 kg) of bombs, air-to-surface missiles, etc.
Status: First identified in 1977, the Su-27 is believed to have entered production at Komsomolsk in 1980–81, initial operational capability having been anticipated early 1985.
Notes: Generally comparable in size and weight to the F-15 Eagle, the Su-27 possesses a broadly similar configuration to that of the MiG-29, but is both larger and heavier. An all-weather counterair fighter with secondary attack capability, the Su-27 is equipped with a track-while-scan radar, a pulse Doppler lookdown/shootdown weapon system, infrared search and tracking and a digital data link. The AA-10 missiles are likely to be supplemented by a 23-mm or 30-mm rotary cannon, and for the attack mission as many as 12 1,102-lb (500 kg) bombs are expected to be carried.

SUKHOI SU-27 (FLANKER)

Dimensions: (Estimated) Span, 46 ft 0 in (14,00 m); length, 60 ft 0 in (21,00 m); wing area, 538 sq ft (50,00 m²).

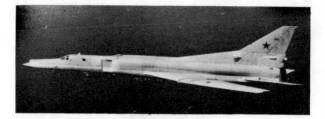

TUPOLEV TU-22M (BACKFIRE-B)

Country of Origin: USSR.

Type: Medium-range strategic bomber and maritime strike/reconnaissance aircraft.

Power Plant: Two (estimated) 33,070 lb st (15 000 kgp) dry and 46,300 lb st (21 000 kgp) reheat Kuznetsov turbofans.

Performance: (Estimated) Max speed (short-period dash), 1,265 mph (2 036 km/h) or Mach=1·91 at 39,370 ft (12 000 m), (sustained), 1,056 mph (1 700 km/h) or Mach=1·6 at 39,370 ft (12 000 m), 685 mph (1 100 km/h) or Mach=0·9 at sea level; combat radius (unrefuelled with single AS-4 ASM and high-altitude subsonic mission profile), 2,610 mls (4 200 km); max unrefuelled combat range (with 12,345 lb/5 600 kg internal ordnance), 3,420 mls (5 500 km).

Weights: (Estimated) Max take-off, 260,000 lb (118 000 kg).

Armament: Remotely-controlled tail barbette housing twin 23-mm NR-23 cannon. Internal load of free-falling weapons up to 12,345 lb (5 600 kg) or one AS-4 Kitchen inertially-guided stand-off missile housed semi-externally.

Status: Flight testing of initial prototype commenced late 1969, with pre-production series of up to 12 aircraft following in 1972–73. Initial version (Backfire-A) was built in small numbers only. Initial operational capability attained with Backfire-B in 1975–76, production rate of 30 annually being attained in 1977 and remaining constant at beginning of 1985, when 145–150 were in service with Soviet Long-range Aviation and a similar quantity with the Soviet Naval Air Force. An advanced version, the Backfire-C, with redesigned engine air intakes and presumably uprated engines has been reported under test, but its production status was uncertain at the beginning of 1985.

TUPOLEV TU-22M (BACKFIRE-B)

Dimensions: (Estimated) Span (20 deg sweep), 115 ft 0 in (35,00 m), (55 deg sweep), 92 ft 0 in (28,00 m); length, 138 ft 0 in (42,00 m); height, 29 ft 6 in (9,00 m); wing area, 1,830 sq ft (170,00 m²).

TUPOLEV (BLACKJACK-A)

Country of Origin: USSR.

Type: Long-range strategic bomber and maritime strike/reconnaissance aircraft.

Power Plant: Four 30,000 lb st (13 610 kgp) dry and 50,000 lb st (22 680 kgp) reheat turbofan.

Performance: (Estimated) Max (over-target dash) speed, 1,380 mph (2 220 km/h) at 40,000 ft (12 200 m), or Mach = 2·09; range cruise, 595 mph (960 km/h) at 45,000 ft (13 720 m), or Mach = 0·9; unrefuelled combat radius, 4,540 mls (7 300 km).

Weights: (Estimated) Empty, 260,000 lb (117 950 kg); max take-off, 590,000 lb (267 625 kg).

Armament: Maximum weapon load (estimated), of 36,000 lb (16 330 kg).

Status: First identified under test (at Ramenskoye) in 1979. Believed to have entered production 1982–83, with initial operational capability anticipated in 1986–7.

Notes: Initially known by the provisional identification designation Ram-P and a product of the Tupolev design bureau, Blackjack-A is apparently some 25 per cent larger than the Rockwell B-1B and is intended as a replacement for the intercontinental attack version of the Tu-95 Bear. It is anticipated that the Soviet Union will build a series of about 100 bombers of this type.

TUPOLEV (BLACKJACK-A)

Dimensions: (Estimated) Span (minimum sweep), 150 ft 0 in (54,00 m), (maximum sweep), 101 ft 0 in (30,75 m); length, 175 ft 0 in (53,35 m); wing area, 2,500 sq ft (232,25 m²).

VALMET L-80 TP

Country of Origin: Finland.

Type: Side-by-side two-seat primary/basic trainer.

Poer Plant: One 360 shp Allison 250-B17D turboprop.

Performance: (Manufacturer's estimates) Max speed, 217 mph (350 km/h) at 9,840 ft (3 000 m); initial climb, 2,065 ft/min (10,49 m/sec); service ceiling (approx), 24,600 ft (7 500 m); range (max fuel and no reserves), 963 mls (1 550 km).

Weights: Empty equipped, 1,852 lb (840 kg); max take-off, 3,968 lb (1 800 kg).

Armament: (Armament training and light strike) Max external ordnance load of 1,323 lb (600 kg) distributed between four wing strongpoints, the inner pair stressed for 551 lb (250 kg) and outer pair for 330·5 lb (150 kg). Typical loads (as single-seater) include four 330·5-lb (150-kg) bombs or two 551-lb (250-kg) bombs plus two flare pods.

Status: Prototype first flown 12 February 1985.

Notes: The L-80 TP owes much to the earlier piston-engined L-70 Miltrainer, 30 of which were delivered as the Vinka (an Arctic wind) to the Finnish Air Force during 1980–82. While primarily intended for the training role, the L-80 TP is adaptable for a variety of other tasks, including observation and liaison and the aeromedical mission (with a single stretcher and one medical attendant) and the cockpit has provision for a second pair of seats.

VALMET L-80 TP

Dimensions: Span, 33 ft 7¾ in (10,25 m); length, 25 ft 10¼ in (7,88 m); height, 10 ft 10 in (3,30 m); wing area, 161·5 sq ft (15,00 m²).

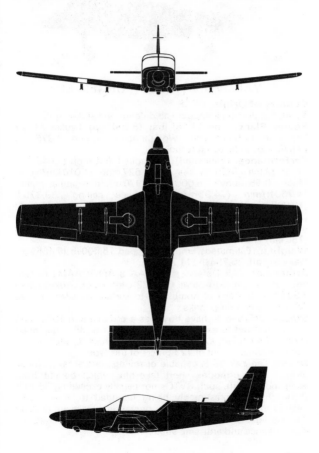

YAKOVLEV YAK-38 (FORGER-A)

Country of Origin: USSR.

Type: Single-seat shipboard air defence and strike fighter.

Power Plant: One 17,985 lb st (8160 kgp) Lyulka AL-21 lift/cruise turbojet and two tandem-mounted 7,875 lb st (3570 kgp) Kolesov lift turbojets.

Performance: (Estimated) Max speed, 648 mph (1042 km/h) or Mach=0·85 at sea level, 627 mph (1010 km/h) or Mach=0·95 above 36,000 ft (10970 m); max initial climb, 14,750 ft/min (74,93 m/sec); service ceiling, 39,375 ft (12000 m); combat radius with max ordnance, 150 mls (240 km) LO-LO-LO, 230 mls (370 km) HI-LO-HI, (air defence with two GSh-23 gun pods and two drop tanks), 115 mls (185 km) with 1 hr 15 min on station.

Weights: (Estimated) Empty equipped 16,500 lb (7485 kg); max take-off, 25,794 lb (11 700 kg).

Armament: (Air Defence) Two AA-8 Aphid AAMs or two podded 23-mm twin-barrel GSh-23 cannon, or (strike) up to 7,936 lb (3600 kg) of bombs, air-to-surface missiles such as AS-7 Kerry and drop tanks.

Status: Believed to have flown as a prototype in 1971, and initially referred to as the Yak-36MP, the Yak-38 is deployed aboard the carriers *Kiev*, *Minsk* and *Novorossisk*, each vessel having a complement of 12 fighters of this type.

Notes: The Yak-38 is capable of rolling vertical take-offs as distinct from orthodox short take-offs which benefit from wing-induced lift, such RVTOs not usually exceeding 35 mph (56 km/h) and presumably being intended to avoid overheating the deck plates. Primary operational tasks are fleet air defence against shadowing maritime surveillance aircraft, reconnaissance and anti-ship strike.

YAKOVLEV YAK-38 (FORGER-A)

Dimensions: (Estimated) Span, 24 ft 7 in (7,50 m); length, 52 ft 6 in (16,00 m); height, 11 ft 0 in (3,35 m); wing area, 199·14 sq ft (18,50 m²).

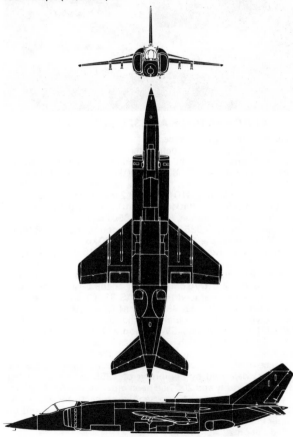

AÉROSPATIALE AS 332L SUPER PUMA

Country of Origin: France.
Type: Medium transport helicopter.
Power Plant: Two 1,755 shp Turboméca Makila turboshafts.
Performance: (At 18,080 lb/8 200 kg) Max speed, 184 mph (296 km/h); max cruise, 173 mph (278 km/h) at sea level; max inclined climb. 1,810 ft/min (9,2 m/sec); hovering ceiling (in ground effect), 9,840 ft (3 000 m), (out of ground effect), 7,545 ft (2 300 m); range, 527 mls (850 km).
Weights: Empty, 9,635 lb (4 370 kg); normal loaded, 18,080 lb (8 200 kg); max take-off, 19,840 lb (9 000 kg).
Dimensions: Rotor diam, 49 ft 5¾ in (15,08 m); fuselage length, 48 ft 7¾ in (14,82 m).
Notes: First flown on 10 October 1980, the AS 332L is a stretched (by 2·5 ft/76 cm) version of the basic Super Puma which is being produced in civil (AS 332C) and military (AS 332B) versions. The AS 332L and M (illustrated) are respectively civil and military variants of the stretched model, and the AS 332F is a navalised ASW version with an overall length of 42 ft 1½ in (12,83 m) with rotor blades folded. Deliveries of the AS 332C began in October 1981 with the AS 332L following in December. One hundred and fourteen Super Pumas (all versions) delivered by beginning of 1985, when production was four monthly and 200 had been ordered. The AS 332B and C carry 20 troops and 17 passengers respectively. Eleven AS 332s have been assembled by Nurtanio in Indonesia and the Super Puma is now being built as the NAS-332, the first being rolled out on 22 April 1984.

AEROSPATIALE AS 350 ECUREUIL

Country of Origin: France.
Type: Six-seat light general-purpose utility helicopter.
Power Plant: (AS 350B) One 641 shp Turboméca Arriel, or (AS 350D) 615 shp Avco Lycoming LTS 101-600A2 turbo-shaft.
Performance: (AS 350B) Max speed, 169 mph (272 km/h) at sea level; cruise, 144 mph (232 km/h); max inclined climb, 1,555 ft/min (7,9 m/sec); hovering ceiling (in ground effect), 9,678 ft (2 950 m), (out of ground effect), 7,382 ft (2 250 m); range, 435 mls (700 km) at sea level.
Weights: Empty, 2,348 lb (1 065 kg); max take-off, 4,630 lb (2 100 kg).
Dimensions: Rotor diam, 35 ft 0¾ in (10,69 m); fuselage length (tail rotor included), 35 ft 9½ in (10,91 m).
Notes: The first Ecureuil (Squirrel) was flown on 27 June 1974 (with an LTS 101 turboshaft) and the second on 14 February 1975 (with an Arriel). The LTS 101-powered version (AS 350D) is being marketed in the USA as the AStar. By the beginning of 1985, production rate of both versions combined was running at 15 monthly, with 766 delivered and 993 ordered. The standard Ecureuil is a six-seater and features include composite rotor blades, a so-called Starflex rotor head, simplified dynamic machinery and modular assemblies to simplify changes in the field. The AS 350D AStar version is assembled and finished by Aérospatiale Helicopter at Grand Prairie, Alberta. Ecureuils are being assembled in Brazil as the HB 350B Esquilo.

AEROSPATIALE AS 355F ECUREUIL 2

Country of Origin: France.

Type: Six-seat light general-purpose utility helicopter.

Power Plant: Two 420 shp Allison 250-C20F turboshafts.

Performance: Max speed, 169 mph (272 km/h) at sea level; max. cruise, 144 mph (232 km/h) at sea level; max inclined climb, 1,614 ft/min (8,2 m/sec); hovering ceiling (out of ground effect), 7,900 ft (2 410 m); service ceiling, 14,800 ft (4 510 m); range, 470 mls (756 km) at sea level.

Weights: Empty, 2,778 lb (1 260 kg); max take-off, 5,292 lb (2 400 kg).

Dimensions: Rotor diam, 35 ft 0¾ in (10,69 m); fuselage length (tail rotor included), 35 ft 9½ in (10,91 m).

Notes: Flown for the first time on 27 September 1979, the Ecureuil 2 employs an essentially similar airframe and similar dynamic components to those of the single-engined AS 350 Ecureuil (see page 217), and is intended primarily for the North American market on which it is known as the TwinStar. Deliveries of the Ecureuil 2/TwinStar commenced in July 1981. From the first quarter of 1982, the production model has been the AS 355F which has higher max take-off weight than the AS 355E that it has succeeded. The AS 355F has main rotor blades of increased chord, twin-body servo command units and two electrical generators. Total of 287 delivered by beginning of 1985 against orders for 498. The AS 355M (illustrated) is an armed military model, 50 examples of which have been ordered by the *Armée de l'Air*. A TOW installation is available for the anti-armour role.

AÉROSPATIALE SA 365 DAUPHIN 2

Country of Origin: France.
Type: Multi-purpose and transport helicopter.
Power Plant: Two 700 shp Turboméca Arriel 1 C turboshafts.
Performance: (SA 365N) Max speed, 190 mph (305 km/h); max continuous cruise, 173 mph (278 km/h) at sea level; max inclined climb, 1,279 ft/min (6,5 m/sec); hovering ceiling (in ground effect), 3,296 ft (1 005 m), (out of ground effect), 3,116 ft (950 m); range, 548 mls (882 km) at sea level.
Weights: Empty, 4,288 lb (1 945 kg); max take-off, 8,487 lb (3 850 kg).
Dimensions: Rotor diam, 39 ft 1½ in (11,93 m); fuselage length (including tail rotor), 37 ft 6⅓ in (11,44 m).
Notes: Flown as a prototype on 31 March 1979, the SA 365 is the latest derivative of the basic Dauphin (see 1982 edition), and is being manufactured in four versions, the 10–14-seat commercial SA 365N, the military SA 365M (illustrated above) which can transport 13 commandos and carry eight HOT missiles, the navalised SA 365F with folding rotor, Agrion radar and four AS 15TT anti-ship missiles (20 ordered by Saudi Arabia for delivery from 1984) and the SA 366G, an Avco Lycoming LTS 101-750-powered search and rescue version for the US Coast Guard as the HH-65A Seaguard. Ninety of the last version are being procured by the US Coast Guard, with completion in 1985. Production of the SA 365N was 5–7 monthly at the beginning of 1985 when 198 had been delivered against total orders for 346 Dauphin helicopters (all versions).

AGUSTA A 109A MK II

Country of Origin: Italy.
Type: Eight-seat light utility helicopter.
Power Plant: Two 420 shp Allison 250-C20B turboshafts.
Performance: (At 5,402 lb/2 450 kg) Max speed, 193 mph (311 km/h); max continuous cruise, 173 mph (278 km/h); range cruise, 143 mph (231 km/h); max inclined climb rate, 1,820 ft/min (9,25 m/sec); hovering ceiling (in ground effect), 9,800 ft (2 987 m), (out of ground effect), 6,800 ft (2 073 m); max range, 356 mls (573 km).
Weights: Empty equipped, 3,125 lb (1 418 kg); max take-off, 5,730 lb (2 600 kg).
Dimensions: Rotor diam, 36 ft 1 in (11,00 m); fuselage length, 35 ft 2½ in (10,73 m).
Notes: The A 109A Mk II is an improved model of the basic A 109A, the first of four prototypes of which flew on 4 August 1971, with customer deliveries commencing late 1976. Some 260 A 109As had been ordered by the beginning of 1985. The Mk II, which supplanted the initial model in production during 1981, has been the subject of numerous detail improvements, the transmission rating of the combined engines being increased from 692 to 740 shp, and the maximum continuous rating of each engine from 385 to 420 shp. An anti-armour version has been procured by Argentine, Libyan and Yugoslav forces. In 1984, a "widebody" version of the A 109 Mk II was introduced. Flown in September of that year, this has new side panels adding 8 in (20 cm) to the cabin width.

AGUSTA A 109K

Country of Origin: Italy.

Type: Light military utility helicopter.

Power Plant: Two 700 shp Turboméca Arriel 1K turboshafts.

Performance: Max speed (clean), 193 mph (311 km/h) at sea level; max cruise, 168 mph (270 km/h) at sea level; max inclined climb rate, 1,820 ft/min (9,2 m/sec); hovering ceiling (out of ground effect), 15,300 ft (4 665 m); ferry range, 460 mls (740 km).

Weights: Empty, 3,515 lb (1 595 kg); max take-off, 6,285 lb (2 850 kg).

Dimensions: Rotor diam, 36 ft 1 in (11,00 m); fuselage length, 36 ft 6 in (11,11 m).

Notes: The A 109K is a re-engined, military derivative of the A 109A Mk II (see page 220) optimised for hot and high conditions. A prototype of the A 109K was flown in April 1983, with a more representative second prototype following in March 1984. Apart from the engines, the A 109K differs from earlier models in having a fixed undercarriage and more advanced avionics. It can accommodate up to seven troops or two casualty stretchers and two medical attendants in the medevac role. Weapons may be carried on four attachment points and typically comprise four outrigger-mounted TOW or six HOT anti-armour missiles, 7,62-mm machine gun pods, or 12-tube (2,75-in/70-mm) or seven-tube (3,2-in/81-mm) rocket pods. Versions equipped for search and rescue are proposed.

AGUSTA A 129 MANGUSTA

Country of Origin: Italy.
Type: Two-seat light attack helicopter.
Power Plant: Two 915 shp Rolls-Royce Gem 2 Mk 1004D turboshafts.
Performance: (Estimated) Max speed, 173 mph (278 km/h); cruise (TOW configuration at 8,377 lb/3 800 kg), 149 mph (240 km/h) at 5,740 ft (1 750 m); max inclined climb (at 8,377 lb/3 800 kg), 2,087 ft/min (10,6 m/sec); hovering ceiling at 8,090 lb/3 670 kg), (in ground effect), 10,795 ft (3 290 m), (out of ground effect), 7,840 ft (2 390 m).
Weights: Mission, 8,080 lb (3 665 kg); max take-off, 8,377 lb (3 800 kg).
Dimensions: Rotor diam, 39 ft 0½ in (11,90 m); fuselage length, 40 ft 3¼ in (12,27 m).
Notes: The A 129 Mangusta (Mongoose) dedicated attack and anti-armour helicopter with full night/bad weather combat capability has been developed to an Italian Army requirement. The first of four flying prototypes commenced flight test on 15 September 1983, and first deliveries are scheduled for 1987, with 66 expected to be funded for the Italian Army. In typical anti-armour configuration, the A 129 will be armed with eight TOW missiles to which can be added 2·75-in (7-cm) rocket launchers for suppressive fire. The fourth prototype, flown in March 1985, has a unified electronic control system, combining flight controls, and weapon aiming and firing systems.

AGUSTA-SIKORSKY AS 61N1 SILVER

Country of Origin: Italy (USA).
Type: Commercial transport helicopter.
Power Plant: Two 1,500 shp General Electric CT58-140-1/2 turboshafts.
Performanece: Max speed, 150 mph (241 km/h) at 2,000 ft (610 m); cruise, 139 mph (224 km/h) at sea level; max inclined climb, 1,300 ft/min (6,6 m/sec); hovering ceiling (in ground effect), 8,700 ft (2 650 m), (out of ground effect), 3,800 ft (1 160 m); operating radius (10 passengers or 2,000 lb/907 kg plus reserves), 316 mls (510 km).
Weights: Max take-off (internal load), 21,000 lb (9 525 kg), (external load), 22,500 lb (10 205 kg).
Dimensions: Rotor diam, 62 ft 0 in (18,90 m); fuselage length, 58 ft 11$\frac{1}{2}$ in (17,97 m).
Notes: Flown for the first time as a prototype on 25 July 1984, the AS 61N1 Silver is an Agusta derivative of the Sikorsky S-61N, production of which terminated in 1980. The production rights to the S-61N were acquired by Agusta, the principal differences of the Silver being a shorter (by 4 ft 2 in/1,27 m) fuselage and an increase in internal fuel capacity. Twenty-two to 28 passengers may be carried and the helicopted may be rapidly converted for cargo transport. The Silver is intended primarily for offshore oil rig support, and, at the beginning of 1985, consideration was being given to a version with 1,760 shp General Electric CT7 turboshafts, but no production decision had been taken.

BELL AH-1S HUEYCOBRA

Country of Origin: USA.

Type: Two-seat light attack helicopter.

Power Plant: One 1,800 shp Avco Lycoming T53-L-703 turboshaft.

Performance: Max speed, 172 mph (277 km/h), (TOW configuration), 141 mph (227 km/h); max inclined climb, 1,620 ft/min (8,23 m/sec); hovering ceiling TOW configuration (in ground effect), 12,200 ft (3 720 m); max range, 357 mls (574 km).

Weights: (TOW configuration) Operational empty, 6,479 lb (2 939 kg); max take-off, 10,000 lb (4 535 kg).

Dimensions: Rotor diam, 44 ft 0 in (13,41 m); fuselage length, 44 ft 7 in (13,59 m).

Notes: The AH-1S is a dedicated attack and anti-armour helicopter serving primarily with the US Army which had received 297 new-production AH-1S HueyCobras by mid-1981, plus 290 resulting from the conversion of earlier AH-1G and AH-1Q HueyCobras. Current planning calls for conversion of a further 372 AH-1Gs to AH-1S standards, and both conversion and new-production AH-1S HueyCobras are being progressively upgraded to "Modernised AH-1S" standard, the entire programme being scheduled for completion in 1985, resulting in a total of 959 "Modernised" AH-1S Huey-Cobras. In December 1979, one YAH-1S was flown with a four-bladed main rotor as the Model 249. The AH-1S is being licence-built in Japan by Fuji for the Ground Self-Defence Force which is to receive 54 examples.

BELL AH-1T+ SUPERCOBRA

Country of Origin: USA.

Type: Two-seat light attack helicopter.

Power Plant: Two 1,693 shp General Electric T700-GE-401 turboshafts.

Performance: Max cruising speed, 184 mph (296 km/h) at 3,000 ft (915 m); hovering ceiling (out of ground effect), 10,000 ft (3 050 m); range, 380 mls (611 km) at 3,000 ft (915 m).

Weights: Empty, 9,700 lb (4 400 kg); max take-off, 14,750 lb (6 691 kg).

Dimensions: Rotor diam, 48 ft 0 in (14,63 m); fuselage length, 45 ft 3 in (13,79 m).

Notes: Flown for the first time on 16 November 1983, the AH-1T+ SuperCobra is an enhanced-capability derivative of the AH-1T SeaCobra (see 1984 edition) of the US Marine Corps. The first of an initial batch of 22 SuperCobras is scheduled to be delivered to the USMC in March 1986, and a follow-on batch of a further 22 is anticipated. More powerful and more heavily armed than the SeaCobra, the primary USMC mission of the SuperCobra will be to provide escort for troop-carrying helicopters, and in this role it can augment its 20-mm three-barrel rotary cannon with up to four AIM-9L Sidewinder missiles on the stub-wing pylons. A typical load for the anti-armour mission can comprise eight laser-guided Hellfire launch-and-leave missiles, other weapon options including 76 2·75-in (70-mm) unguided rockets, two GPU-2A 20-mm gun pods or 16 5-in (12,7-mm) Zuni rockets.

BELL MODEL 214ST

Country of Origin: USA.

Type: Medium transport helicopter (20 seats).

Power Plant: Two 1,625 shp (limited to combined output of 2,250 shp) General Electric CT7-2A turboshafts.

Performance: Max cruising speed, 164 mph (264 km/h) at sea level, 161 mph (259 km/h) at 4,000 ft (1 220 m); hovering ceiling (in ground effect), 12,600 ft (3 840 m), (out of ground effect), 3,300 ft (1 005 m); range (standard fuel), 460 mls (740 km).

Weights: Max take-off (internal or external load), 17,500 lb (7 938 kg).

Dimensions: Rotor diam, 52 ft 0 in (15,85 m); fuselage length, 50 ft 0 in (15,24 m).

Notes: The Model 214ST (Super Transport) is a significantly improved derivative of the Model 214B BigLifter (see 1978 edition), production of which was phased out early 1981, initial customer deliveries of the Model 214ST beginning early 1982. The Model 214ST test-bed was first flown in March 1977, and the first of three representative prototypes (one in military configuration and two for commercial certification) commenced its test programme in August 1979. Work on an initial series of 100 helicopters of this type commenced in 1981. A version with wheel landing gear was certificated in March 1983, and alternative layouts are available for either 16 or 17 passengers. Military operators include the Venezuelan and Peruvian air forces, and the Royal Thai Army, an example in service with the last-mentioned force being illustrated above.

BELL MODEL 222B

Country of Origin: USA.

Type: Eight/ten-seat light utility and transport helicopter.

Power Plant: Two 680 shp Avco Lycoming LTS 101-750C-1 turboshafts.

Performance: Max cruising speed, 150 mph (241 km/h) at sea level, 146 mph (235 km/h) at 8,000 ft (2 400 m); max climb, 1,730 ft/min (8,8 m/sec); hovering ceiling (in ground effect), 10,300 ft (3 135 m), (out of ground effect), 6,400 ft (1 940 m); range (no reserves), 450 mls (724 km) at 8,000 ft (2 400 m).

Weights: Empty equipped, 4,577 lb (2 076 kg); max take-off (standard configuration), 8,250 lb (3 742 kg).

Dimensions: Rotor diam, 42 ft 0 in (12,80 m); fuselage length, 39 ft 9 in (12,12 m).

Notes: The first of five prototypes of the Model 222 was flown on 13 August 1976, an initial production series of 250 helicopters of this type being initiated in 1978, with production deliveries commencing in January 1980, and some 230 delivered by beginning of 1985, when production rate was two monthly. Several versions of the Model 222 are on offer or under development, these including an executive version with a flight crew of two and five or six passengers, and the so-called "offshore" model with accommodation for eight passengers and a flight crew of two. Options include interchangeable skids. The Model 222B has a larger main rotor and uprated power plant, a utility version, the Model 222UT, having been certificated mid 1983.

BELL MODEL 400 TWINRANGER

Country of Origin: USA (Canada).
Type: Multi-purpose seven-seat light helicopter.
Power Plant: Two 420 shp Allison 250-C20 turboshafts.
Performance: (Manufacturer's estimates) Max cruising
speed, 161 mph (259 km/h); hovering ceiling (out of ground
effect), 7,600 ft (2 315 m); max range, 450+ mls (724+ km).
Weights: Empty, 3,075 lb (1 395 kg); max take-off, 5,500 lb
(2 495 kg).
Dimensions: Rotor diam, 35 ft 0 in (10,67 m).
Notes: The Model 400 TwinRanger, the first prototype of
which was flown on 4 July 1984, is the first of a new family
of commercial and military single- and twin-engined helicopters, this including the Model 400A with a 1,000 shp Pratt &
Whitney (Canada) PW209T turboshaft and the Model 440
which will employ composites for some of its major components. This family of helicopters is to be manufactured by a
new Bell facility in Canada under a contract with the
Canadian government, and customer deliveries are expected
to commence (Model 400) in 1986. The Model 400A is due
to fly in 1987, and will become available in the spring of
1989, and the Model 440 is to fly late 1988, with customer
deliveries commencing in the following year. During the initial
stages of the Canadian programme, the rotor heads, rotor
blades, transmission systems and other complex components
will be manufactured in the USA, the Canadian plant building
the airframes and undertaking final assembly.

BELL MODEL 406 (OH-58D)

Country of Origin: USA.
Type: Two-seat scout helicopter.
Power Plant: One 650 shp Allison 250-C30R turboshaft.
Performance: Max speed, 147 mph (237 km/h) at 4,000 ft (1 220 m); max cruise, 138 mph (222 km/h) at 2,000 ft (610 m); max inclined climb, 1,540 ft/min (7,82 m/sec); hovering ceiling (in ground effect), 12,000+ ft (3 660+ m), (out of ground effect), 11,200 ft (3 415 m); range (no reserves), 345 mls (556 km).
Weights: (Manufacturer's estimates) Empty, 2,825 lb (1 281 kg); max take-off, 4,500 lb (2 041 kg).
Dimensions: Rotor diam, 35 ft 0 in (10,67 m); fuselage length, 33 ft 10 in (10,31 m).
Notes: The Model 406 proposal was winning contender in the AHIP (Army Helicopter Improvement Program) competition, the first of five prototypes having flown on 6 October 1983. US Army development and operational tests were scheduled to be completed in March 1985, and current planning calls for the modification of at least 578 existing OH-58A Kiowa helicopters to OH-58D standards during 1985–91. The OH-58D features a mast-mounted sight, specialised avionics and an integrated multiplex cockpit. Armed with two air-to-air missiles, the OH-58D is intended as a close-combat reconnaissance helicopter which can support attack helicopter missions and direct artillery fire as well as perform intelligence gathering and surveillance missions.

BELL MODEL 406CS (COMBAT SCOUT)

Country of Origin: USA.
Type: Light two/five-seat combat helicopter.
Power Plant: One 650 shp Allison 250-C30R turboshaft.
Performance: Max speed, 143 mph (230 km/h); max cruise, 138 mph (222 km/h); hovering ceiling (in ground effect), 14,000 ft (4 267 m), (out of ground effect), 10,700 ft (3 260 m); max range, 288 mls (463 km).
Weights: Empty, 2,732 lb (1 239 kg); max take-off, 4,500 lb (2 041 kg).
Dimensions: Rotor diam, 35 ft 0 in (10,67 m); fuselage length, 33 ft 10 in (10,31 m).
Notes: The Model 406CS Combat Scout is fundamentally a simplified derivative of the Model 406 AHIP (see page 229), retaining the dynamics and drive train. Featuring folding rotor blades and collapsible undercarriage to facilitate air transportation, the Combat Scout offers a wide variety of armament options. Four TOW 2 missiles can be carried for the anti-armour role, or a mix of air-to-air missiles, 7,62-mm gun pods and 2·75-in (70-mm) rocket pods. Armour protection for the engine, fuel tanks and crew is optional, and any current roof-mounted sight may be fitted. The Model 406 is a progressive development of the Model 206 JetRanger series (see 1984 edition), more than 7,500 example of which have been delivered (all versions) and for which a manufacturing licence is held by Agusta. The Model 406CS entered flight test summer 1985 and deliveries are offered for 1986.

BELL MODEL 412

Country of Origin: USA.
Type: Fifteen-seat utility transport helicopter.
Power Plant: One 1,800 shp Pratt & Whitney PT6T-3B-1 turboshaft.
Performance: Max speed, 149 mph (240 km/h) at sea level; cruise, 143 mph (230 km/h) at sea level, 146 mph (235 km/h) at 5,000 ft (1 525 m); hovering ceiling (in ground effect), 10,800 ft (3 290 m), (out of ground effect), 7,100 ft (2 165 m) at 10,500 lb/4 763 kg; max range, 282 mls (454 km), (with auxiliary tanks), 518 mls (834 km).
Weights: Empty equipped, 6,535 lb (2 964 kg); max take-off, 11,900 lb (5 397 kg).
Dimensions: Rotor diam, 46 ft 0 in (14,02 m); fuselage length, 41 ft 8½ in (12,70 m).
Notes: The Model 412, flown for the first time in August 1979, is an updated Model 212 (production of which was continuing at the beginning of 1985) with a new-design four-bladed rotor, a shorter rotor mast assembly, and uprated engine and transmission systems, giving more than twice the life of the Model 212 units. Composite rotor blades are used and the rotor head incorporates elastomeric bearings and dampers to simplify moving parts. An initial series of 200 helicopters was laid down with customer deliveries commencing February 1981. Licence manufacture is undertaken by Agusta in Italy, a military version being designated AB 412 Griffon, and is also to be undertaken by Nurtanio in Indonesia.

BOEING VERTOL 414 CHINOOK

Country of Origin: USA.
Type: Medium transport helicopter.
Power Plant: Two 3,750 shp Avco Lycoming T55-L-712 turboshafts.
Performance: (At 45,400 lb/20 593 kg) Max speed, 146 mph (235 km/h) at sea level; average cruise, 131 mph (211 km/h); max inclined climb, 1,380 ft/min (7,0 m/sec); service ceiling, 8,400 ft (2 560 m); max ferry range, 1,190 mls (1 915 km).
Weights: Empty, 22,591 lb (10 247 kg); max take-off, 50,000 lb (22 680 kg).
Dimensions: Rotor diam (each), 60 ft 0 in (18,29 m); fuselage length, 51 ft 0 in (15,55 m).
Notes: The Model 414 as supplied to the RAF as the Chinook HC Mk 1 combines some features of the US Army's CH-47D (see 1980 edition) and features of the Canadian CH-147, but with provision for glassfibre/carbonfibre rotor blades. The first of 33 Chinook HC Mk 1s for the RAF was flown on 23 March 1980 and accepted on 2 December 1980, with deliveries continuing through 1981, three more being ordered in 1982 and five in 1983. The RAF version can accommodate 44 troops and has three external cargo hooks. During 1981, Boeing Vertol initiated the conversion to essentially similar CH-47D standards a total of 436 CH-47As, Bs and Cs, and this programme is continuing throughout 1985. Licence manufacture of the Chinook has been undertaken in Italy. Eighteen Model 414s have been purchased by the Spanish Army.

HUGHES 500MD DEFENDER II

Country of Origin: USA.

Type: Light gunship and multi-role helicopter.

Power Plant: One 420 shp Allison 250-C20B turboshaft.

Performance: (At 3,000 lb/1 362 kg) Max speed, 175 mph (282 km/h) at sea level; cruise, 160 mph (257 km/h) at 4,000 ft (1 220 m); max inclined climb, 1,920 ft/min (9,75 m/sec); hovering ceiling (in ground effect), 8,800 ft (2 682 m), (out of ground effect), 7,100 ft (2 164 m); max range, 263 mls (423 km).

Weights: Empty, 1,295 lb (588 kg); max take-off (internal load), 3,000 lb (1 362 kg), (with external load), 3,620 lb (1 642 kg).

Dimensions: Rotor diam, 26 ft 5 in (8,05 m); fuselage length, 21 ft 5 in (6,52 m).

Notes: The Defender II multi-mission version of the Model 500MD was introduced mid-1980 for 1982 delivery, and features a Martin Marietta rotor mast-top sight, a General Dynamics twin-Stinger air-to-air missile pod, an underfuselage 30-mm chain gun and a pilot's night vision sensor. The Defender II can be rapidly reconfigured for anti-armour target designation, anti-helicopter, suppressive fire and transport roles. The Model 500MD TOW Defender (carrying four tube-launched optically-tracked wire-guided anti-armour missiles) is currently in service with Israel (30), South Korea (45) and Kenya (15). Production of the 500 was seven monthly at the beginning of 1985, when an upgraded version, the Model 500ME, was being introduced.

233

HUGHES 530F

Country of Origin: USA.
Type: Five-seat light utility helicopter.
Power Plant: One 650 shp Allison 250-C30 turboshaft.
Performance: Max cruise speed, 155 mph (250 km/h) at sea level, econ cruise, 150 mph (241 km/h) at 5,000 ft (1 525 m); max inclined climb, 1,780 ft/min (9,04 m/sec); hovering ceiling (in ground effect), 12,000 ft (3 660 m), (out of ground effect), 9,600 ft (2 925 m); range, 269 mls (434 km) at 5,000 ft (1 525 m).
Weights: Max take-off, 3,100 lb (1 406 kg).
Dimensions: Rotor diam, 27 ft 6 in (8,38 m); fuselage length, 23 ft 2½ in (7,07 m).
Notes: The Model 530F is the "hot and high" variant of the Model 500E (see 1983 edition) which is characterised by a longer, recontoured nose compared with the preceding Model 500D, offering increased leg room for front seat occupants and a 12 per cent increase in headroom for rear seat passengers. The principal difference between the Models 500E and 530F is the power plant, the former having a 520 shp 250-C20B. The Model 500E was flown on 28 January 1982, and was certificated in November 1982, and the Model 530F was flown in October 1982. Customer deliveries of the Model 530F began in January 1984, and on the following 4 May a military version, the Model 530MG, entered flight test, this being intended primarily for the light attack mission and being essentially similar to the 500ME apart from power plant.

HUGHES AH-64 APACHE

Country of Origin: USA.
Type: Tandem two-seat attack helicopter.
Power Plant: Two 1,690 shp General Electric T700-GE-701 turboshafts.
Performance: Max speed, 191 mph (307 km/h); cruise, 179 mph (288 km/h); max inclined climb, 3,200 ft/min (16,27 m/sec); hovering ceiling (in ground effect), 14,600 ft (4 453 m), (outside ground effect), 11,800 ft (3 600 m); service ceiling, 8,000 ft (2 400 m); max range, 424 mls (682 km).
Weights: Empty, 9,900 lb (4 490 kg); primary mission, 13,600 lb (6 169 kg); max take-off, 17,400 lb (7 892 kg).
Dimensions: Rotor diam, 48 ft 0 in (14,63 m); fuselage length, 48 ft 1⅞ in (14,70 m).
Notes: Winning contender in the US Army's AAH (Advanced Attack Helicopter) contest, the YAH-64 flew for the first time on 30 September 1975. Two prototypes were used for the initial trials, the first of three more with fully integrated weapons systems commenced trials on 31 October 1979, a further three following in 1980. Planned total procurement comprises 675 AH-64s through 1990, with 171 ordered by beginning of 1985, and a peak production rate of 12 monthly, deliveries having commenced during the summer of 1984. The AH-64 is armed with a single-barrel 30-mm gun based on the chain-driven bolt system and suspended beneath the forward fuselage, and eight BGM-71A TOW or 16 Hellfire laser-seeking missiles may be carried.

KAMOV KA-27 (HELIX)

Country of Origin: USSR.
Type: Shipboard anti-submarine warfare helicopter.
Power Plant: Two 2,225 shp Isotov TV3-117V turboshafts.
Performance: (Estimated) Max speed, 160 mph (260 km/h) at sea level; normal cruise, 130 mph (209 km/h); max range, 600 mls (965 km); range with 11,023 lb (5 000 kg) payload, 112 mls (180 km).
Weights: (Estimated) Normal loaded, 20,000-21,000 lb (9 070-9 525 kg).
Dimensions: (Estimated) Rotor diam (each), 55 ft (16,75 m); fuselage length, 36 ft 1 in (11,00 m).
Notes: Retaining the pod-and-boom fuselage configuration and superimposed co-axial rotor arrangement of the Ka-25 Hormone (see 1984 Edition), the Ka-27 was first seen during Zapad-81 exercises held by WarPac forces in the Baltic in September 1981, and is believed to have flown in prototype form in 1979–80. Developed in both shipboard ASW and civil freight transportation versions simultaneously (the latter as the Ka-32), the Ka-27 is larger and more powerful than the preceding Kamov helicopter which it is intended to supplant in Soviet Naval service, its greater internal capacity suggesting that an alternative mission to ASW may be that of assault troop transport for operation from *Berezina*-class replenishment ships. Basic ASW version is known to NATO as Helix-A, a missile target acquisition and midcourse guidance version being Helix-B.

MBB BO 105LS

Country of Origin: Federal Germany.
Type: Five/six-seat light utility helicopter.
Power Plant: Two 550 shp Allison 250-C28C turboshafts.
Performance: Max speed, 168 mph (270 km/h) at sea level; max cruise, 157 mph (252 km/h) at sea level; max climb, 1,970 ft/min (10 m/sec); hovering ceiling (in ground effect), 13,120 ft (4 000 m), (out of ground effect), 11,280 ft (3 440 m); range, 286 mls (460 km).
Weights: Empty, 2,756 lb (1 250 kg); max take-off, 5,291 lb (2 400 kg), (with external load), 5,512 lb (2 500 kg).
Dimensions: Rotor diam, 32 ft 3½ in (9,84 m); fuselage length, 28 ft 1 in (8,56 m).
Notes: The BO 105LS is a derivative of the BO 105CB (see 1979 edition) with uprated transmission and more powerful turboshaft for "hot-and-high" conditions. It is otherwise similar to the BO 105CBS Twin Jet II (420 shp Allison 250-C20B) which was continuing in production at the beginning of 1985, when some 1,056 BO 105s (all versions) had been delivered and production was running at five monthly, and licence assembly has been undertaken in Indonesia, the Philippines and Spain. Deliveries to the Federal German Army of 227 BO 105M helicopters for liaison and observation tasks commenced late 1979, and deliveries of 212 HOT-equipped BO 105Ps for the anti-armour role began on 4 December 1980 and were completed mid-1984. The latter have uprated engines and transmission systems.

MBB-KAWASAKI BK 117

Countries of Origin: Federal Germany and Japan.
Type: Multi-purpose eight-to-twelve-seat helicopter.
Power Plant: Two 600 shp Avco Lycoming LTS 101-650B-1 turboshafts.
Performance: Max speed, 171 mph (275 km/h) at sea level; cruise, 164 mph (264 km/h) at sea level; max climb, 1,970 ft/min (10 m/sec); hovering ceiling (in ground effect), 13,450 ft (4100 m), (out of ground effect), 10,340 ft (3150 m); range (max payload), 339 mls (545,4 km).
Weights: Empty, 3,351 lb (1 520 kg); max take-off, 6,173 lb (2 800 kg).
Dimensions: Rotor diam, 36 ft 1 in (11,00 m); fuselage length, 32 ft 5 in (9,88 m).
Notes: The BK 117 is a co-operative development between Messerschmitt-Bölkow-Blohm and Kawasaki, the first of two flying prototypes commencing its flight test programme on 13 June 1979 (in Germany), with the second following on 10 August (in Japan). A decision to proceed with series production was taken in 1980, with first flying on 24 December 1981, and production deliveries commencing first quarter of 1983 in which year 20 were delivered. A further 20 were built in 1984, and production tempo was two monthly at the beginning of 1985. MBB is responsible for the main and tail rotor systems, tail unit and hydraulic components, while Kawasaki is responsible for production of the fuselage, undercarriage and transmission.

MIL MI-8 (HIP)

Country of Origin: USSR.
Type: Assault transport helicopter.
Power Plant: Two 1,700 shp Isotov TV2-117A turboshafts.
Performance: Max speed, 161 mph (260 km/h) at 3,280 ft (1 000 m), 155 mph (250 km/h) at sea level; max cruise, 140 mph (225 km/h); hovering ceiling (in ground effect), 6,233 ft (1 900 m), (out of ground effect), 2,625 ft (800 m); range (standard fuel), 290 mls (465 km).
Weights: (Hip-C) Empty, 14,603 lb (6 624 kg); normal loaded, 24,470 lb (11 100 kg); max take-off, 26,455 lb (12 000 kg).
Dimensions: Rotor diam, 69 ft 10¼ in (21,29 m); fuselage length, 60 ft 0¾ in (18,31 m).
Notes: Currently being manufactured at a rate of 700–800 annually, with more than 7,500 delivered for civil and military use since its debut in 1961, the Mi-8 is numerically the most important Soviet helicopter. Current military versions include the Hip-C basic assault transport, the Hip-D and -G with additional antennae and podded equipment for airborne communications, the Hip-E and the Hip-F, the former carrying up to six rocket pods and four Swatter IR-homing anti-armour missiles, and the latter carrying six Sagger wire-guided anti-armour missiles, and the Hip-J (illustrated) and -K ECM variants. The Mi-8 can accommodate 24 troops or 12 stretchers, and most have a 12,7-mm machine gun in the nose. An enhanced version, the Mi-17, is described on page 241.

MIL MI-14PL (HAZE-A)

Country of Origin: USSR.
Type: Amphibious anti-submarine helicopter.
Power Plant: Two 1,900 shp Isotov TV-3 turboshafts.
Performance: (Estimated) Max speed, 143 mph (230 km/h); max cruise, 130 mph (210 km/h); hovering ceiling (in ground effect), 5,250 ft (1 600 m), (out of ground effect), 2,295 ft (700 m); tactical radius, 124 mls (200 km).
Weights: (Estimated) Max take-off, 26,455 lb (12 000 kg).
Dimensions: Rotor diam, 69 ft 10¼ in (21,29 m); fuselage length, 59 ft 7 in (18,15 m).
Notes: The Mi-14PL amphibious anti-submarine warfare helicopter, which serves with shore-based elements of the Soviet Naval Air Force, is a derivative of the Mi-8 (see page 239) with essentially similar power plant and dynamic components to those of the later Mi-17, and much of the structure is common between the two helicopters. New features include the boat-type hull, outriggers which, housing the retractable lateral twin-wheel undercarriage members, incorporate water rudders, a search radar installation beneath the nose and a sonar "bird" beneath the tailboom root. The Haze-B is a version of the Mi-14PL used for the mine countermeasures task. The Mi-14PL possesses a weapons bay for ASW torpedoes, nuclear depth charges and other stores. This amphibious helicopter reportedly entered service in 1975 and about 120 were in Soviet Navy service by the beginning of 1985, other recipients being Bulgaria, Libya, Cuba, Poland and East Germany.

MIL MI-17 (HIP-H)

Country of Origin: USSR.
Type: Medium transport helicopter.
Power Plant: Two 1,900 shp Isotov TV3-117MT turbo-shafts.
Performance: (At 28,660 lb/13 000 kg) Max speed, 162 mph (260 km/h); max continuous cruise, 149 mph (240 km/h) at sea level; hovering ceiling (at 24,250 lb/ 11 000 kg out of ground effect), 5,800 ft (1 770 m); max range, 590 mls (950 km).
Weights: Empty, 15,652 lb (7 100 kg); normal loaded, 24,250 lb (11 000 kg); max take-off, 28,660 lb (13 000 kg).
Dimensions: Rotor diam, 69 ft 10$\frac{1}{4}$ in (21,29 m); fuselage length, 60 ft 5$\frac{1}{4}$ in (18,42 m).
Notes: The Mi-17 medium-lift helicopter is essentially a more powerful and modernised derivative of the late fifties technology Mi-8 (see page 239). The airframe and rotor are fundamentally unchanged, apart from some structural re-inforcement of the former, but higher-performance turboshafts afford double the normal climb rate and out-of-ground-effect hover ceiling of the earlier helicopter, and increase permissible maximum take-off weight. The Mi-17 has a crew of two-three and can accommodate 24 passengers, 12 casualty stretchers or up to 8,818 lb (4 000 kg) of freight. Externally, the Mi-17 is virtually indistinguishable from its precursor, the Mi-8, apart from marginally shorter engine nacelles and port-side tail rotor. The military version is known as Hip-H, India and Cuba being recent recipients of this version.

MIL MI-24 (HIND-D)

Country of Origin: USSR.

Type: Assault and anti-armour helicopter.

Power Plant: Two 2,200 shp Isotov TV3-117 turboshafts.

Performance: (Estimated) Max speed, 170–180 mph (273–290 km/h) at 3,280 ft (1 000 m); max cruise, 145 mph (233 km/h); max inclined climb rate, 3,000 ft/min (15,24 m/sec).

Weights: (Estimated) Normal take-off, 22,000 lb (10 000 kg).

Dimensions: (Estimated) Rotor diam, 55 ft 0 in (16,76 m); fuselage length, 55 ft 6 in (16,90 m).

Notes: By comparison with the Hind-A version of the Mi-24 (see 1977 edition), the Hind-D embodies a redesigned forward fuselage and is optimised for the gunship role, having tandem stations for the weapons operator (in nose) and pilot. The Hind-D can accommodate eight fully-equipped troops, has a barbette-mounted four-barrel rotary-type 12,7-mm cannon beneath the nose and can carry up to 2,800 lb (1 275 kg) of ordnance externally, including four AT-2 Swatter IR-homing anti-armour missiles and four pods each with 32 57-mm rockets. It has been exported to Afghanistan, Algeria, Bulgaria, Cuba, Czechoslovakia, East Germany, Hungary, Iraq, Libya, Poland and South Yemen. The Hind-E is similar but has provision for four laser-homing tube-launched Spiral anti-armour missiles, may be fitted with a twin-barrel 23-mm cannon on the starboard side of the fuselage and embodies some structural hardening, steel and titanium being substituted for aluminium in certain critical components.

MIL MI-26 (HALO)

Country of Origin: USSR.

Type: Military and commercial heavy-lift helicopter.

Power Plant: Two 11,400 shp Lotarev D-136 turboshafts.

Performance: Max speed, 183 mph (295 km/h); normal cruise, 158 mph (255 km/h); hovering ceiling (in ground effect), 14,765 ft (4 500 m), (out of ground effect), 5,905 ft (1 800 m); range (at 109,127 lb/49 500 kg), 310 mls (500 km), (at 123,457 lb/56 000 kg), 497 mls (800 km).

Weights: Empty, 62,169 lb (28 200 kg); normal loaded, 109,227 lb (49 500 kg); max take-off, 123,457 lb (56 000 kg).

Dimensions: Rotor diam, 104 ft 11⅞ in (32,00 m); fuselage length (nose to tail rotor), 110 ft 7¾ in (33,73 m).

Notes: The heaviest and most powerful helicopter ever flown, the Mi-26 first flew as a prototype on 14 December 1977, production of pre-series machines commencing in 1980, and preparations for full-scale production having begun in 1981. Featuring an innovative eight-bladed main rotor and carrying a flight crew of five, the Mi-26 has a max internal payload of 44,090 lb (20 000 kg). The freight hold is larger than that of the fixed-wing Antonov An-12 transport and at least 70 combat-equipped troops or 40 casualty stretchers can be accommodated. Although allegedly developed to a civil requirement, the primary role of the Mi-26 is obviously military and the Soviet Air Force achieved initial operational capability with the series version late 1983. During the course of 1982, the Mi-26 established new international payload-to-height records. Ten Mi-26 helicopters are to be supplied to the Indian Air Force during 1985.

243

SIKORSKY CH-53E SUPER STALLION

Country of Origin: USA.
Type: Amphibious assault transport helicopter.
Power Plant: Three 4,380 shp General Electric T64-GE-415 turboshafts.
Performance: (At 56,000 lb/25 400 kg) Max speed, 196 mph (315 km/h) at sea level; cruise, 173 mph (278 km/h) at sea level; max inclined climb, 2,750 ft/min (13,97 m/sec); hovering ceiling (in ground effect), 11,550 ft (3 520 m), (out of ground effect), 9,500 ft (2 895 m); range, 1,290 mls (2 075 km).
Weights: Empty, 33,226 lb (15 071 kg); max take-off, 73,500 lb (33 339 kg).
Dimensions: Rotor diam, 79 ft 0 in (24,08 m); fuselage length, 73 ft 5 in (22,38 m).
Notes: The CH-53E is a growth version of the CH-53D Sea Stallion (see 1974 edition) embodying a third engine, an uprated transmission system, a seventh main rotor blade and increased rotor diameter. The first of two prototypes was flown on 1 March 1974, and the first of two pre-production examples followed on 8 December 1975, production of two per month being divided between the US Navy and US Marine Corps at beginning of 1985, against total requirement for 160 through 1992. The CH-53E can accommodate up to 55 troops in a high-density seating arrangement. Fleet deliveries began mid-1981, and the first pre-production example of the MH-53E mine countermeasures version, 57 of which are required by the US Navy, flew September 1983.

SIKORSKY S-70 (UH-60A) BLACK HAWK

Country of Origin: USA.

Type: Tactical transport helicopter.

Power Plant: Two 1,543 shp General Electric T700-GE-700 turboshafts.

Performance: Max speed, 224 mph (360 km/h) at sea level; cruise, 166 mph (267 km/h); vertical climb rate, 450 ft/min (2,28 m/sec); hovering ceiling (in ground effect), 10,000 ft (3 048 m), (out of ground effect), 5,800 ft (1 758 m); endurance, 2·3-3·0 hrs.

Weights: Design gross, 16,500 lb (7 485 kg); max take-off, 22,000 lb (9 979 kg).

Dimensions: Rotor diam, 53 ft 8 in (16,23 m); fuselage length, 50 ft 0¾ in (15,26 m).

Notes: The Black Hawk was winner of the US Army's UTTAS (Utility Tactical Transport Aircraft System) contest. The first of three YUH-60As was flown on 17 October 1974, and a company-funded fourth prototype flew on 23 May 1975. The Black Hawk is primarily a combat assault squad carrier, accommodating 11 fully-equipped troops. Variants under development at the beginning of 1985 were the EH-60A ECM model and the HH-60A Night Hawk rescue helicopter (see page 246). The USAF is expected to procure 90 HH-60s and 77 EH-60s. The first production deliveries of the UH-60A to the US Army were made in June 1979, with some 635 delivered by beginning of 1985 against requirement for 1,107. S-70A export version has been selected by the Israeli Air Force as its new medium transport and utility helicopter.

SIKORSKY S-70 (HH-60A) NIGHT HAWK

Country of Origin: USA.
Type: All-weather combat rescue helicopter.
Power Plant: Two 1,543 shp General Electric T700-GE-700 turboshafts.
Performance: Max speed, 167 mph (268 km/h) at sea level; max cruise, 147 mph (238 km/h) at 4,000 ft (1 220 m); hovering ceiling (in ground effect), 9,500 ft (2 895 m), (out of ground effect), 5,600 ft (1 705 m); endurance (max fuel), 4 hr 51 min.
Weights: Empty, 12,642 lb (5 734 kg); max take-off (mission), 20,413 lb (9 259 kg), (alternative), 22,000 lb (9 979 kg).
Dimensions: Rotor diam, 53 ft 8 in (16,36 m); fuselage length (excluding refuelling probe), 50 ft 0¾ in (15,26 m).
Notes: The HH-60A Night Hawk is an optimised USAF rescue version of the US Army's UH-60A Black Hawk intended to undertake unescorted day/night missions at treetop level over a radius of 287 miles (463 km) from a friendly base without flight refuelling. The prototype was flown on 4 February 1984, and the USAF plans to procure 90 Night Hawks with deliveries commencing in 1988, the series model having T700-GE-401 turboshafts rated at 1,690 shp. Accommodation is provided for a crew of two and 10 passengers, or four litters and three seated casualties/medical attendants. Defensive equipment will include 7,62-mm machine guns, a radar warning receiver, a flare/chaff dispenser and an infra-red jammer.

SIKORSKY S-70C

Country of Origin: USA.
Type: Commercial transport helicopter.
Power Plant: Two 1,625 shp General Electric CT7-2C turboshafts.
Performance: Econ cruise speed, 186 mph (300 km/h); max inclined climb rate, 2,770 ft/min (14,1 m/sec); service ceiling, 17,200 ft (5,240 m); hovering ceiling (in ground effect), 8,700 ft (2 650 m), (out of ground effect), 4,800 ft (1 460 m); range (standard fuel with reserves), 294 mls (473 km) at 155 mph (250 km/h) at 3,000 ft (915 m), (max fuel without reserves), 342 mls (550 km).
Weights: Empty, 10,158 lb (4 607 kg); max take-off, 20,250 lb (9 185 kg).
Dimensions: Rotor diam, 53 ft 8 in (16,36 m); fuselage length, 50 ft 0¾ in (15,26 m).
Notes: The S-70C is a commercial derivative of the H-60 series of military helicopters, and may be configured for a variety of utility missions, such as maritime and environmental survey, mineral exploration and external lift, provision being made for an 8,000-lb (3 629-kg) capacity external cargo hook. Options include a winterisation kit, a cabin-mounted rescue hoist and an aeromedical evacuation kit. The S-70C has a flight deck crew of two and can accommodate 12 passengers in standard cabin configuration or up to 19 passengers in high density layout. Twenty-four were being delivered to China at the beginning of 1985.

SIKORSKY S-70L (SH-60B) SEA HAWK

Country of Origin: USA.
Type: Shipboard multi-role helicopter.
Power Plant: Two 1,690 shp General Electric T700-GE-401 turboshafts.
Performance: (At 20,244 lb/9 183 kg) Max speed, 167 mph (269 km/h) at sea level; max cruising speed, 155 mph (249 km/h) at 5,000 ft (1 525 m); max vertical climb, 1,192 ft/min (6,05 m/sec); time on station (at radius of 57 mls/92 km), 3 hrs 52 min.
Weights: Empty equipped, 13,678 lb (6 204 kg); max take-off, 21,844 lb (9 908 kg).
Dimensions: Rotor diam, 53 ft 8 in (16,36 m); fuselage length, 50 ft 0¾ in (15,26 m).
Notes: Winner of the US Navy's LAMPS (Light Airborne Multi-Purpose System) Mk III helicopter contest, the SH-60B is intended to fulfil both anti-submarine warfare (ASW) and anti-ship surveillance and targeting (ASST) missions, and the first of five prototypes was flown on 12 December 1979, and the last on 14 July 1980. Evolved from the UH-60A (see page 245), the SH-60B is intended to serve aboard DD-963 destroyers, DDG-47 Aegis cruisers and FFG-7 guided-missile frigates as an integral extension of the sensor and weapon system of the launching vessel. The US Navy has a requirement for 204 SH-60Bs, the first of which was delivered in October 1983, and for 175 simplified SH-60Fs without MAD gear.

SIKORSKY S-76B

Country of Origin: USA.

Type: Commercial transport helicopter.

Power Plant: Two 960 shp Pratt & Whitney (Canada) PT6B-36 turboshafts.

Performance: (Manufacturer's estimates) Max cruise speed, 167 mph (269 km/h); econ cruise, 155 mph (250 km/h); max inclined climb, 1,700 ft/min (8,63 m/sec); service ceiling, 16,000 ft (4 875 m); hovering ceiling (in ground effect), 8,700 ft (2 650 m), (out of ground effect), 5,900 ft (1 800 m); range (max payload), 207 mls (333 km), (max standard fuel), 414 mls (667 km).

Weights: Empty, 6,250 lb (2 835 kg); max take-off, 11,000 lb (4 989 kg).

Dimensions: Rotor diam, 44 ft 0 in (13,41 m); fuselage length, 43 ft 4½ in (13,22 m).

Notes: The S-76B is a derivative of the S-76 Mk II (see 1984 edition) from which it differs primarily in the type of power plant. A prototype of the S-76B was flown for the first time on 22 June 1984, and first customer deliveries are scheduled for the first half of 1985. Offering a 51 per cent increase in useful load under hot and high conditions by comparison with the S-76 Mk II, the S-76B provides accommodation for a flight crew of two and a maximum of 12 passengers. A total of some 270 S-76 helicopters (all versions) had been delivered by the beginning of 1985. Commercial and military (AUH-76) utility versions are available.

WESTLAND SEA KING

Country of Origin: United Kingdom (US licence).

Type: Anti-submarine warfare and search-and-rescue helicopter.

Power Plant: Two 1,660 shp Rolls-Royce Gnome H.1400-1 turboshafts.

Performance: Max speed, 143 mph (230 km/h); max continuous cruise at sea level, 131 mph (211 km/h); hovering ceiling (in ground effect), 5,000 ft (1 525 m), (out of ground effect), 3,200 ft (975 m); range (standard fuel), 764 mls (1 230 km), (auxiliary fuel), 937 mls (1 507 km).

Weights: Empty equipped (ASW), 13,672 lb (6 201 kg), (SAR), 12,376 lb (5 613 kg); max take-off, 21,000 lb (9 525 kg).

Dimensions: Rotor diam, 62 ft 0 in (18,90 m); fuselage length, 55 ft 9¾ in (17,01 m).

Notes: The Sea King Mk 2 is an uprated version of the basic ASW and SAR derivative of the licence-built S-61D (see 1982 edition), the first Mk 2 being flown on 30 June 1974, and being one of 10 Sea King Mk 50s ordered by the Australian Navy. Twenty-one to the Royal Navy as HAS Mk 2s, and 19 examples of a SAR version to the RAF as HAR Mk 3s. Current production version is the HAS Mk 5, delivery of 17 to Royal Navy having commenced October 1980, and a further 13 subsequently being ordered. All HAS Mk 2s being brought up to Mk 5 standards and eight Mks 2 and 3 fitted with Thorn-EMI searchwater radar for airborne early warning duty.

WESTLAND LYNX 3

Country of Origin: United Kingdom.
Type: Two-seat anti-armour helicopter.
Power Plant: Two 1,115 shp Rolls-Royce Gem 60 turbo-shafts.
Performance: (Manufacturer's estimates) Max speed, 190 mph (306 km/h) at sea level; cruise, 172 mph (278 km/h); range (max fuel and 20 min reserves), 385 mls (620 km); endurance, 3·5 hrs.
Weights: Normal max take-off, 13,000 lb (5 896 kg).
Dimensions: Rotor diam, 42 ft 0 in (12,80 m); length (main rotor folded), 45 ft 3 in (13,79 m).
Notes: Derived from the earlier production Lynx (see 1984 edition), the Lynx 3 is a dedicated anti-armour helicopter, a prototype of which flew for the first time on 14 June 1984. Incorporating the dynamic systems of the earlier versions of the Lynx, it is engineered to afford increased survivability and can mount greater firepower. Suitable for day or night operation and in adverse weather conditions, the Lynx 3 can be armed with Stinger missiles for self defence, and can carry and launch Euromissile HOT, Hughes TOW and Rockwell Hellfire anti-armour missiles. It can also be equipped with a 20-mm cannon and a pintle-mounted 7,62-mm machine gun. The crew seats are provided with armour protection. A naval version has been proposed with 360-deg radar, MAD, dunking sonar, active and passive sonobuoys, and torpedoes, depth charges or Sea Skua missiles.

WESTLAND 30-100

Country of Origin: United Kingdom.

Type: Transport and utility helicopter.

Power Plant: Two 1,265 shp Rolls-Royce Gem 60-1 turboshafts.

Performance: Max speed (at 10,500 lb/4 763 kg), 163 mph (263 km/h) at 3,000 ft (915 m); hovering ceiling (in ground effect), 7,200 ft (2 195 m), (out of ground effect), 5,000 ft (1 525 m); range (seven passengers), 426 mls (686 km).

Weights: Operational empty (typical), 6,880 lb (3 120 kg); max take-off, 12,800 lb (5 806 kg).

Dimensions: Rotor diam, 43 ft 8 in (13,31 m); fuselage length, 47 ft 0 in (14,33 m).

Notes: The WG 30, flown for the first time on 10 April 1979, is a private venture development of the Lynx (see 1984 edition) featuring an entirely new fuselage offering a substantial increase in capacity. Aimed primarily at the multi-role military helicopter field, the WG 30 has a crew of two and in the transport role can carry 17–22 passengers. Commitment to the WG 30 at the time of closing for press covers initial production of 41, deliveries of which began January 1982. British Airways has purchased two and four have been supplied to the US-based Airspur Airline, other US purchasers including SFO Helicopter Airlines and Helicopter Hire. The WG 30 utilises more than 85% of the proven systems of the WG 13 Lynx, and the WG 30-200 (flown on 3 September 1983) differs from the -100 in having General Electric CT7-2 turboshafts.

INDEX OF AIRCRAFT TYPES